From Alcatraz to Africa

Hope you enjoy the book!

Jon Konnerup

JONATHAN KONNERUP

ISBN 978-1-64258-194-2 (paperback)
ISBN 978-1-64258-195-9 (digital)

Christian Faith Publishing, Inc.
832 Park Avenue
Meadville, PA 16335
www.christianfaithpublishing.com

Printed in the United States of America

Endorsements

Jon Konnerup's account of his family's call to Africa and the difficulties of pioneer mission work in a primitive setting is the fascinating story of missionary sacrifice during the turbulent years of the communist takeover in Ethiopia. From Alcatraz to Africa is a non-fiction adventure story and an inspiring record of the work of pioneer Baptist Bible Fellowship missionary families.

Bill Monroe
Pastor of Florence Baptist Temple
Florence, SC

Finally, this remarkable story is being told. I first met Richard and Jeannine outside of Nairobi in 1979. This book will take you on their incredible journey into East Africa. From political wars, to family heartbreaks, to their persevering faith. You will come away inspired by how two ordinary people can accomplish extraordinary things. From Alcatraz to Africa is a must read.

Marty Mosley
RightNow Media
Allen, TX

Growing up in a strong BBFI missions-minded church, the missionaries in this book were legends to me. As a pastor's wife for many years, I've had the privilege of personally meeting some of these heroes. I'm thankful Jon has recorded these stories so future generations can understand the hardships and victories of walking a faith-filled life with Jesus Christ. It's never a dull moment, and always worth any sacrifice or hardship. Sit back and enjoy your trip to Africa!

Donna Braymer
Pastor's wife/Business editor of Harrison Daily Times
Harrison, AR

This book is Jon's tribute to his family! From the family's initial faith to their long missionary service, we learn of their sacrificial love for Jesus Christ and the world He challenged us to impact. It is a loving recognition of the earlier days of missions and the brave men and women who served their Lord no matter the costs. Amazing story!

Dr. Jerry Thorpe
Grandbury, TX

This book does a great job of giving an 'inside look' at the exciting and faith stretching journey of every missionary family. It's an incredible story of commitment and passion that gives an eye-opening look at missions. It will inspire you and encourage you to be grateful for the path missionaries travel to get to the field!

Jon Slayden
Pastor of Second Baptist Church
Midland, TX

Contents

Preface

This book, *From Alcatraz to Africa*, tells the fascinating story of how God used the Konnerup family for His glory. It is the story of how my parents came to Jesus, met each other, and together answered the call of God to be missionaries in Ethiopia. Most of the story took place in the northern part of Ethiopia from 1960 to 1976. There are five kids in our family. We went through many experiences, some of which were harrowing, funny, and yet others, totally amazing. While this story consists of my personal memories, it is sprinkled with other memories told by family members and fellow missionaries.

While reading this book, I hope you will recognize the watch care, protection, and leading of God in our lives. Without Him, none of this would have been possible. Over the course of the book, you will see the importance of the prayers of the many believers in our supporting churches in America. It was their prayers that kept my family going and encouraged during the hardships of being pioneer missionaries. I pray this book will challenge others to give their lives to serve God as missionaries and to trust in Him to care for and enable them in that service. In addition, I want to encourage believers to keep praying for missionaries. You may never know the difference that your consistent and persistent prayers make all around the world. Missionaries rely on your prayers! Don't stop praying!

This book is dedicated to my mom and dad, Jeannine and Richard Konnerup. These two are more than my parents—they are my heroes. They were willing to go when and where God called them. They went to a difficult place to help the people know what Jesus had done for them on the cross of Calvary. They went to a primitive place, lived in challenging situations, and sacrificed in so many ways all for the glory of God. I never heard Mom or Dad complain of their situation or question God's call upon their lives. The thing that has always impressed me about my parents is that they never spoke negatively about the people or the country of Ethiopia and the hardships they faced. They knew what God wanted them to do, and they did it. It was their call from God that kept them on the field no matter what difficulties came their way.

As you read this book, you will realize there were many times they could have complained or given up on the ministry. You will read of some difficult situations they encountered. You will read of some amazing things God did through them and how He provided for them.

I am proud to be the son of Richard and Jeannine Konnerup. I thank God for the privilege of growing up as a missionary kid. I praise God for allowing me to have parents who love Jesus and serve Him no matter what may come. To observe them love and serve God firsthand has had a huge impact upon my life. May God use me as He has used them in the harvest.

"The Spirit of the Lord GOD *is* upon me; because the LORD hath anointed me to preach good tidings unto the meek; he hath sent me to bind up the brokenhearted, to proclaim liberty to the captives, and the opening of the prison to *them that are* bound" (Isaiah 61:1).

CHAPTER ONE

Alcatraz

Clarence Preshaw was assigned guard duty in the kitchen and mess hall in the prison, known as Alcatraz. Although Clarence was a nice person, he was a tough guard who could not be bribed or fooled. His nickname among the prisoners was Pressure. He was one of three guards watching over the prisoners as they ate. He was responsible for policing the mess hall, kitchen, basement, and the bakery. Things had been quite calm with the prisoners on that day. It almost seemed too calm. As he walked through the door from the mess hall into the kitchen, he was jumped by three prisoners who had grabbed a couple of knives and a pair of scissors.

As two prisoners held him down, the third one stabbed Clarence in the chest and stomach thirteen times before the other two guards and backup guards made it to the kitchen. Not only had he been stabbed, they also cut off part of his nose. After subduing the prisoners, they rushed him to the clinic on the island.

You can imagine the concern for Clarence's wife and three kids—Ralph, Marilyn, and Jeannine. The doctors told the family that no vital organs or blood vessels had been punctured or lacerated. They were amazed that more deadly damage had not been done. This was great news to the family and a huge relief. Clarence recovered fully from these wounds after being in the infirmary for three months.

Upon his return to duty, Clarence was reassigned to be a guard at the lighthouse to watch for any escape attempts by the prisoners. The guards on Alcatraz knew it was dangerous to work there because the most hardened and notorious of the criminal prisoners in American history were often sent there.

The federal prison on Alcatraz Island is in the middle of the chilly waters of California's San Francisco Bay. Among those who served time at the maximum-security facility were the infamous gangsters Al "Scarface" Capone, murderer Robert "Birdman of Alcatraz" Stroud, and George "Machine Gun" Kelly. The average number of inmates housed in the prison was around 260. Usually, they were so dangerous that the train cars in which they were transported were put on barges and taken to the island from San Francisco. From the dock on Alcatraz, the prisoners would be taken directly to their cell.

Although Alcatraz is most famous for being a prison, it was also considered home for many officers and guards, in addition to their wives and children. Approximately three hundred civilians lived on the island with sixty to eighty children. They all knew each other, and it was like a small-town community. It was known as a "small town with a big jail."

Jeannine liked living there. It was kind of a novelty when people heard you lived there. Their apartment was in the prison guard complex where most of the other families lived. It was close enough to the main prison building, that on many nights she could hear the prisoners yelling and banging on their bars. She never got to have a pet dog or cat because they weren't allowed on the island. Everyone knew everyone, and usually, life was normal—until her dad was attacked. This brought things back to reality for Jeannine, as her parents often reminded them of the dangers on the island.

The mothers worried about their kids, not so much because of the prisoners but because there were not that many places to play. They feared the kids wandering down to the edge of the island where there were cliffs and big rocks. There were no beaches, and the water was rough and cold. Like most adventurous kids, these dangerous places were where the kids often went. They were especially warned about playing on the west side of the island since anyone seen climbing around the rocks might be mistaken for an escaping prisoner and be shot.

The authorities claimed that no prisoner "successfully escaped from the island" despite some claims to the contrary. Through the years, there were fourteen escape attempts. One such failed attempt occurred in 1946 and is known as the Battle of Alcatraz. Six prisoners took guards as hostages. Thankfully, the Preshaw family was not on the island when this occurred.

There were things to do that the families could enjoy. They had their own two-lane bowling alley, soda fountain shop, a small convenience store, and the post office. There was a handball court, and they played baseball on the concrete parade ground. Jeannine really liked to play jump-rope with the other kids her age. They flew kites and often played "guards and cons." The older kids could play billiards and even fish off the dock.

Jeannine always enjoyed the ride to school. She would line up with the other school-age kids at the dock each morning and board the boat to San Francisco. Jeannine was in kindergarten. She always sat between her older siblings, brother Ralph and sister Marilyn. The return home was usually tense because the winds seemed to kick up the waves and made it rough in the afternoons.

Families did their primary shopping on the mainland. The prison boat made twelve scheduled runs a day, which made it convenient for school and shopping. Jeannine loved it when the family would go to San Francisco for dinner, though that didn't happen often. It was a special event.

Every Christmas Eve, they sang carols at the warden's home and then sang to prisoners from outside the cellblock building. Jeannine thought it was neat when she would yell out "Merry Christmas" to the prisoners, and they would yell back the same to her.

One day, Clarence came home after filling in for the day in the prison cells area. Jeannine noticed her dad was a little shaken as he told his wife of what happened that day. One of the well-known prisoners, Al Capone, was fighting another prisoner in the shower room. Her dad went to stop them, and Al Capone smarted off back to him and wouldn't stop. Clarence went to him, knocked Capone down with a punch, and told the men to stop fighting. Clarence was known for his no-nonsense attitude, and therefore the nickname

Pressure. The family was nervous for a while because they wondered if Al Capone would have his henchmen on the outside do something to her dad and family when they were in San Francisco away from the island.

Clarence Preshaw is my grandfather. His youngest child, Jeannine, is my mom. It's amazing to think that my mom really did live on Alcatraz. My grandpa never talked much about his time there when we would ask questions. Mom shared these experiences with us. She wasn't around the prisoners much but from time to time they would be out working and would speak to the kids through the fence.

Once she fell while playing and cut herself. They rushed her to the infirmary by taking a shortcut down through the center of the cellblock building. She heard many of the prisoners yelling obscenities as they passed by. She was more afraid of being close to them than the injury she had sustained. It was a frightening experience.

So how did a little girl who lived on Alcatraz Island end up in Africa? Continue to read this book and find out.

CHAPTER TWO

According to God's Plan

B efore that little girl, Jeannine, was born, her family lived in Salt Lake City, Utah. Clarence Preshaw worked for the US government as a treasury agent during the depression era. Jeannine was born on December 6, 1931. Soon thereafter, Clarence went to work as a guard in various penitentiaries. That is how he eventually came to work at one of the most famous prisons called Alcatraz Island in California. In addition to his work on California's infamous Alcatraz Island, he worked as a prison guard on Terminal Island.

After his time working on Alcatraz, Clarence was transferred to Colorado as a treasury agent. He worked with the Alcohol Tax Unit and would run down bootleggers during the prohibition days. On one occasion, he was tracking some bootleggers and came across the house that served as their home base. He crawled through a basement window to get into the house to await their return. When he heard them come in the house, he hurried to hide under a bunch of clothes and blankets. The people's dog came down the stairs and lay down right on top of the pile of clothes and blankets. Every time he would move to shift around, the dog would growl. Eventually, he safely escaped. On other occasions, he dressed like a woman, went down to skid row and into bars to check their alcohol content. It was a dangerous job.

Later, my grandpa Preshaw became an undercover agent and joined the Colorado Mafia in Denver. It was a daring job, but to him, all of this was exciting. When the leader of the Mafia needed a chauffeur, he chose the person he trusted the most—Clarence Preshaw. After some time, my grandpa arrested him, and the mobster told him, "You were the only one around here that I trusted."

The Lord protected Clarence in all these risky jobs. He was grateful to know that the Savior he trusted in was always watching over him. Clarence was known to be a good father who loved his three children. He loved to spend time with them in between these unusual and hazardous assignments. My mom spent her teenage years in Denver, Colorado.

Her dad took them to church as much as he could. Her mother had grown up in the Christian Science cult. It is not believed that her mother ever trusted in Christ as her Savior. My grandma went to church with them sometimes but did not show interest in the Bible. My grandpa encouraged my mom to attend the Englewood Baptist Tabernacle in Englewood, Colorado, which was just a few blocks from their home. As she grew up in the church, she became very active in the youth group.

My dad's story begins with immigrants arriving from Denmark. Olaf Konnerup arrived in the United States as a five-year-old boy with his parents in 1911. Ingeborg Christiansen also arrived in the United States with her parents in 1911 as a baby. Upon their arrival, both families spent one week on Ellis Island under quarantine, which was the rule of that day.

Olaf's family ended up moving across the country and first settled in Nebraska. His father was a blacksmith. A few years later, they moved to Denver, Colorado, when Olaf was in his teenage years. This is where he met Ingeborg, who had just finished high school. They grew up attending a Danish Lutheran church in Denver. They taught the Bible, and as young people, they went through the church's catechisms. Olaf even did some teaching as a young person in that church. However, neither Olaf nor Ingeborg knew the Lord as Savior and did not live for Him either. They later got married in 1929. Their first child was born in Denver on January 24, 1930. He is my dad, Richard Konnerup.

The local Lutheran church had different kid's clubs and social works in the Konnerup's neighborhood. My grandparents sent Dad and his two sisters to those activities. Their church moved about one and a half miles away, and so Dad rode his bike to church. His parents even bought him a suit to wear to church. Later, the church moved farther away, and he could no longer attend.

My grandpa, Olaf Konnerup, was a bricklayer in Denver. However, oftentimes, he would leave and go to Texas and other states to work while the family stayed in Denver. They lived in a double-car garage built out of brick. It was divided into three rooms with a living room, a kitchen, and a bedroom. My two aunts, Joan and Dorothy, were born while living in this house, and they slept in the same bedroom with their parents. Dad slept in the attic in a Morris (fold-down) chair. It had wooden arms, but the back lay down, so it kind of made into a bed for him. The house was heated by a pot-bellied stove. It was a nice, comfortable home that brought many happy family memories. My grandma was mainly a mother and wife, but she also did different kinds of work, such as working in a greenhouse growing flowers and plants. She also cleaned houses for other people on occasion. Both of my grandparents were hardworking, which was a good example to their kids.

It was in junior high that Dad met Johnny Wolfslager, who would become very important in Dad's life. Dad liked sports a lot, and all the boys would get together and play volleyball. Dad and Johnny could beat all the other teams in the neighborhood. He especially liked track and won a lot of blue ribbons for all the races he won. Football was a lot of fun for him too. He scored a lot of touchdowns on kickoffs because he was so fast. Baseball was another competitive sport for the neighborhood boys to enjoy. Dad also played basketball in the nearby church league.

When he finished junior high school, he went to South High School on the south side of Denver. Early on, he made the junior varsity football team and was planning to move up to the varsity team. For some reason though, he decided not to play anymore and went to work for Montgomery Ward part-time wrapping packages for eighty cents an hour. Throughout those years, he remained friends with Johnny, who continually invited him to go to church at Englewood Baptist Tabernacle.

Finally, Dad agreed to go since they were good friends. It was several miles away, but Johnny's mother drove them to Sunday school and church almost every Sunday. When she couldn't transport them, they took the streetcar, which was a long ride. He enjoyed the youth group very much. Dad appreciated the deacons who helped lead the group because of their personal care and concern for the young people. They would all pile into one of the deacon's cars to go on visitation. He would say there were too many of them for the car, but they didn't care and kept piling in. The youth department was very exciting with a lot of activities. Dad really liked the church very much, and the pastor was a strong evangelistic preacher. His name was Harvey Springer.

In 1945, there was an evangelistic meeting that featured a team of two Italian men and their Swedish wives. They were called the Palermo Four. In one of their services, Dad raised his hand during the invitation, admitting he felt the need to be saved from the penalty of his sins and acknowledging he knew he needed Christ as his Savior. Well, after hesitating to go forward and deciding whether to move or not, Harvey Springer, the pastor, walked up to him and said, "Young man, don't you want to go forward and put your trust in the Lord?" So without any further hesitation, Dad made his way forward to the front of the auditorium, and one of the deacons led him to the Lord for salvation. The church was an exciting place where God was moving and working. It grew to over one thousand in attendance.

The youth group was quite active. They didn't have a youth pastor, so the older youth would lead the singing and even do the teaching. One adult, usually a mother of one of the youth, would be there with them. They also met every Sunday evening before the main evening church service. During the week, they would get together for activities that usually consisted of visitation and ministering in nursing homes and retirement centers. They sang for the elderly and even preached to them. Although Dad and Johnny lived far away, they did all they could to participate; soon everything they did for fun was with the youth group. Many of the students in this youth group ended up going to Bible college.

Men like Carl Boonstra, Clifford Clark, Jimmy Strickland, Howard Musgrave, John Sleppy, and Al Wells attribute their interest in ministry to the activities of this youth group. Usually, they held meetings on Saturday and Sunday afternoons on a street corner and preached to the people walking by. Since they were young, the people would wonder what was going on and would end up listening to them. Well, this was good training ground for many who eventually entered the ministry as preachers and missionaries. Jim and Marie Strickland ended up going to Argentina as missionaries. The Musgraves went to Venezuela as missionaries. The Sleppys ended up going to Alaska as missionaries. Many of the others became pastors in America. This youth group even had small singing teams that Mom sang in. One of her best friends was Jeannette Boonstra, Carl's younger sister.

It was in this youth group that my dad met my mom, Jeannine. It is amazing how God had brought them to the same church and youth group from completely different backgrounds. They became close friends and began to date. They didn't have much money, so they would go to the drugstore and have a milkshake. Most of the time, their dates were during a youth group activity. They liked to sit together in church. Mom accepted Christ as her personal Savior as a teenager at Englewood Baptist Tabernacle in 1946. Her Sunday school teacher led her to Christ when she was fifteen. She was baptized by Pastor Harvey Springer. Starting when she was a little girl, a strong desire grew in her heart to be a missionary. She yearned to take the Gospel to China. Mom graduated from Englewood High School in 1949.

My grandpa Konnerup had a big heart for people. He would build a house for a family, and then they would ask him to make changes. He would make those changes and wouldn't even charge them for it. When Dad heard that his mom and dad got saved, his heart overflowed with joy. He thought his dad would probably never be able to tithe because they were in debt to so many people. However, they began immediately to tithe. They put God first, and God began to bless them. They never became rich, but they were able to buy a house for about $18,000. Grandpa Konnerup ended up becoming a deacon in their Baptist church and was very faithful to that ministry. As time went on, the church took up Faith Promise Missions Giving for world missions, and my grandpa gave ten percent tithe and gave ten percent to missions. The church also had a radio program, and he gave another five percent to that radio program. They grew in their Christian life and were faithful to God to the very end of their lives.

My dad became interested in diesel mechanics. One of his high school teachers encouraged him to apply to go to the General Motors school in Indiana. There he could learn to be a diesel engineer to eventually work on locomotives and their engines. Well, one of his good friends in the youth department joined the Navy. Suddenly, the Navy became of interest to my dad as well, and so he joined the Navy in 1948.

He was sent off to boot camp in San Diego, California. He only got off the base one time while he was there. That was because there was an illness going around that prohibited them all from leaving the base. After testing his skills and interests, they determined that he should study electronics. Dad was sent for electronics training in Millington, Tennessee, near Memphis.

Mom and Dad maintained their friendship through correspondence. She did, however, date another young man while Dad was off at boot camp and electronics school. There still seemed to be some interest in each other, and Mom's father even went to visit Dad in Tennessee. However, nothing about marriage was discussed. They were both young but soon became very interested in each other. Once, she even went with her dad to Tennessee, and Dad thought they just came for a normal visit. Her brother and his wife did live in Memphis, and so Dad thought they just came to visit them. However, Mom really went there with the idea that she would hopefully be asked to marry him. Her dad would be there to vouch for her. Unfortunately, Dad did not ask her to marry him, and in fact, he didn't even think about it. He didn't think it was a good time to get married because of their poor financial standing. However, Dad went home for Christmas that year, and at that time, he proposed marriage. She said yes without any hesitation. They got married on June 25, 1949.

Dad was stationed in Corpus Christi, Texas, since he had completed his electronics training. Both of their parents went to Corpus Christi to attend the wedding. The chaplain did not want to marry them because he thought they were too young. Dad was nineteen, and Mom was seventeen. The chaplain said there were too many young people getting married, and many of those unions didn't last. He felt this one wouldn't, either. Somehow, they convinced him to go ahead, and they were married in the chapel on the base in Corpus Christi. Grandpa Konnerup brought a blue 1936 Ford Coupe with them to the wedding and gave it as a wedding present. He had built a single car garage for someone, and the owners paid him with that car.

That Ford had a large trunk in which Mom and Dad could put a bed mattress. The front seats were far enough forward that the mattress fit perfectly in the back and trunk. Every fourth day and every fourth Sunday, Dad had guard duty. Mom wanted to be close by him. So many of those days, she drove the car out to the base, and instead of driving home, she stayed in the parking lot sleeping through the night in the trunk on the mattress. I wonder what the authorities would have done if they ever found out about that.

They did not have much money at all. Once the car would not start, and Dad could not get to work. He realized it needed a new battery. They didn't have enough money to buy one. It was Christmas time, and the chief petty officer from the club came to their trailer and said he had a Christmas gift for them. It was $25. That was enough to buy a battery, and it enabled them to go to church at Christmas. Since they didn't have money to spend, besides purchasing the essentials, they did not go out very much. They stayed home, and one of the things they did a lot was color in coloring books. They each had a coloring book, and they bought one box of crayons. Many evenings they would spend time together coloring pictures in those books. Even later in life, they would do that and remember the early years of their marriage.

While living in Corpus Christi, attending church was very important to them. They had always enjoyed being in the youth department and believed it to be very important to continue in church as a newlywed couple. They faithfully attended the Alameda Baptist Church pastored by Lester Roloff. It was a large church, and they enjoyed it immensely. Lester Roloff was a caring pastor who loved people and spent hours in their homes encouraging, teaching, and praying for them. That example influenced Mom and Dad on how important it is to show the love of Christ through serving others. They thought if the pastor of a large church could do this, surely they could do it as well. They became acquainted with another Navy family, and they went out on visitation together every week. It was during those times of visitation and sitting under the ministry of Lester Roloff that Dad began to consider serving God through a spiritual ministry. He was reminded of his friends in his youth department who had gone off to Bible college studying to be pastors and missionaries. Dad believed God put these things in his mind to begin considering serving the Lord full-time. He began to think that God had brought him and Mom together to be used in some way for His honor and glory. This all must to be according to God's plan, he thought.

They began their married life living in a hotel designated for Navy personnel. However, they didn't have enough money to afford the hotel, so they moved into an eight-by-twelve-foot mobile home. Dad was making $60 a month, and when they got married, they received a family allowance, which increased his salary to $120 a month. In 1950, the government and military passed a law that gave everyone a raise, which amounted to $5 a month. However, they then took away their family allowance and started charging taxes on their income. So his salary went down to nearly $60 a month again. The Navy allowed many to get out of the military if they wanted, and Dad chose to opt out.

He served in the United States Navy between World War II and the Korean War, so he never saw active duty. When they were officially released from the Navy, they moved to Denver, Colorado. Dad learned to work on an altimeter but mostly drew guard duty or cleanup responsibilities. He spent a lot of time guarding planes with all their radios and radars in them. Sometimes they would fly up and down the Mississippi in a beach craft that had a small engine. They learned how to read the radar and use the radios.

After they moved to Denver, Dad began to work for a contractor to learn the trade of bricklayer like his father. He started off working for ninety cents an hour as an apprentice. When winter came, it was very difficult to make a living because of the lack of work. So Dad took a test to get into the Denver Fire Department, and he passed. The pay was $268 a month. Every other day, he had off, and that enabled him to lay brick to help supplement their income.

Another friend named Don Richardson started a church in Boulder, Colorado, about thirty miles north of Denver. Don invited Dad to come up and help him in that ministry. So while he worked for the fire department, which he loved very much, it gave him an opportunity to help his friend with this new ministry in Boulder. He led the singing every other Sunday. Dad was very active in visitation as well. All of this further influenced Dad toward ministry, and he loved it, reaching and serving people.

During those years, Jacque was born in Denver, Colorado, in 1952. A year later, Ole was also born. Ole is short for Olaf, named after our grandpa Konnerup. It is a Danish name. My mom's mother passed away after battling a cancerous tumor in her head. Her dad relocated and lived with my parents for a short time. Some years later, Grandpa Preshaw married again.

CHAPTER THREE

You're Too Old

While Dad was working as a fireman and volunteering in this new ministry in Boulder, Colorado, some pastors in the Denver area had a weekly night school. Dad began attending this to learn more about the Lord and aspects of serving the Lord. Carl Boonstra was one of the teachers, and he was also an associate pastor working with Harvey Springer. Dad and Carl already knew each other, and so it was always good to get together to study and grow in the knowledge of the Word of God. Another one of his friends from the previous youth department was attending this night school. Robert Burkholder was his name, and they all called him Bob.

When the end of the year for the night school came, they held a banquet at the church. On that special night, Dad and his friend Bob were walking on the sidewalk next to the church on their way to the banquet. Carl Boonstra caught up with them and said, "Why don't you fellas stop fooling around and get down to Bible school in Springfield, Missouri?"

Well, Bob agreed and signed up immediately for the next school year. But Dad liked his job as a fireman and didn't want to give it up. It was a very satisfying, exciting, and adventurous job. Carl kept asking Dad about going into the ministry. Dad finally responded and said, "I really want to go to a school where I can learn Greek and Hebrew and all those kinds of things."

Carl responded, "You don't need all that. You just need to get to school and get a little 'spizerinctum' in your life!" He was saying that Dad needed to get "fired up" about the ministry and get on with training and serving. Dad thought about it for an entire year. He sure liked his job with all its activity, and it kept pulling him back.

One day, Dad called Mom on the phone and said they ought to go to Bible school in Springfield, Missouri. He asked her what she thought about that. She did not even pause and said, "Okay, if that's what you want to do." There was no hesitation in her response, and she never questioned how they were going to make a living and take care of their then three kids. Now Dad had to tell the fire chief, who was a Jewish man. When he was told, the chief said, "Well, that is fine if you want to go to school, but I think you better really reconsider this decision."

Dad responded, "I want eighty days of leave in case I don't like it at school so I can come back to my job."

The chief said, "We can't do that."

They discussed this further, and the fire chief finally did agree to give Dad twenty days of leave in case he wanted his job back. Dad remembers thinking back on that and how he knew what God wanted him to do but was hanging on to what felt secure.

Off they went to Springfield, Missouri, from Denver. They had an old pickup truck with a shell on it. They put their furniture and personal things inside. They also had a station wagon. The pickup was hooked up to the Chevy station wagon with a tow bar, and they headed toward Missouri. The three kids got into the car with Mom. The youngest one, Eric, was one month old. He lay in the seat beside Mom while Jacque and Ole sat in the back. Sometimes they would take turns riding with Dad being pulled in the pickup. After only ninety miles outside of Denver, they realized the tow bar was not working. It was too heavy for the car, and the truck behind kept swaying back and forth. They still had over three hundred miles to go. So they unhooked the tow bar and sent the truck back to Denver on the train. They continued the trip in the station wagon. They did not have many of their belongings since they would not all fit in the station wagon. There was no promise of a job, and they went only trusting God to provide.

When they arrived in Springfield, they located a house to rent. Still, there was no income, but they decided to move forward with their plans. They put everything into the house and began to set up with what personal belongings they had. Dad could not find a job in those first weeks. He went to the bricklayer's union, and they said there was not enough work to add him. They said, "Why don't you consider contracting out your own work?" However, he didn't even know where to buy a sack of cement or a wheelbarrow of sand. How was he going to do this without any funds to get started? He kept searching. Finally, at the end of the month, the rent came due, and they could not pay the rent. So they had to move out. The rent was $100 a month. They could not eat and pay that much without a job.

After nonstop searching for another place to live, they found one close to High Street Baptist Church. It was a two-story apartment, and they obtained the lower floor for $45 a month. It was on Prospect Street next door to the house where the landlord's son and daughter-in-law lived. They became special friends with my parents. Sometimes they would bring a meal over for the family. The landlord was an older gentleman who was very kind and understanding. One time, they got three months behind because of not having work. Mr. Thompson said, "Don't tell me your troubles. When you get the money, come and pay me." When Dad got work, he paid the back rent.

Jacque and Ole both went to school at Robberson Elementary School. They kept trying to teach left-handed Ole to write with his right hand, but he couldn't. He kept putting the pencil in his left hand to write. The teacher told Mom and Dad that Ole needed to go get some counseling because he wouldn't use his right hand. They never took him because they didn't have the money.

Dad found a job as a bricklayer making $2.50 an hour, which was one dollar an hour lower than what he made as a bricklayer in Denver. The two bosses, Andy Anderson and Curtis Crane, were great to work for. They understood Dad was attending Bible college in the morning. He would finish his classes and then work from 1:00 p.m. until 4:30 p.m. every day of the week. This worked well until winter came, and the amount of work was reduced.

It was difficult to pay the bills and take care of the needs of the three children. Ole remembers there was a time when they had no money, not even to pay the electric bill. The electricity was turned off, and so they all cuddled together under blankets to stay warm. Thankfully in those days, churches would donate generously to the college, which allowed the students to only pay $25 a month for tuition. In the winter months, Dad went out and shoveled sidewalks to earn extra income. There was one instance when things got very bad and another good friend of his from Colorado, John Aldrich, who was a machinist, found Dad a job in a machine shop. So when he finished classes in the morning, he went to work as a bricklayer as much as he could, and then he would go directly to the machine shop and work there from 5:00 p.m. until midnight. He then returned home and studied for the next day's classes.

In those days, Mom did not go to school. She did attend some classes though to learn what she could. The house next to the current Mission Office parking lot was a nursery. That is where she took Eric while she went to class. Mom and Dad liked their professors who loved preparing students for future ministry. Dr. and Mrs. Gillming, Dr. Eli Harju and Dr. Ross especially impacted them with their teaching and Bible knowledge. Well-known pastors like G. B. Vick and John Rawlings would preach inspiring messages in chapel, challenging the students to make a difference in this world for the Lord. They were all very inspirational.

Dad and Mom attended High Street Baptist Church those three years while in Springfield. They thought Pastor Bill Dowell was a wonderful pastor and that he took the Lord's work very seriously. This greatly influenced them. The Victory Sunday school class led by Earl Smith was their class. They went on visitation every Thursday night. Mr. Smith looked out for them. He was very friendly to them, and they built a lasting relationship with him and his wife. The church ran over 2,500 in attendance, and it was known to have one of the largest Sunday schools in the state of Missouri.

During the summer months, they traveled back to Denver to visit the families and try to lay brick to make more money for when they returned to Springfield. Going back and forth, they drove through small towns. They would drive around in each town praying and looking to see what the need might be for a church there.

Carl Boonstra had left Englewood Baptist Tabernacle to start a new church in another part of Denver. He started East Side Baptist Church. It was doing well right from the start through evangelism and discipleship. Many people were responding to their need for salvation. One summer when Dad and Mom were visiting the Denver area, they met up with Carl. He asked, "Why are you going to these small towns to see what is needed? You can come here and go a mile down the road from our church, and there are ten thousand people that we are not going to be able to reach." He encouraged them to return to Denver and start a church. This got Dad to think about starting a church in Denver, and he prayed about this since he felt God was leading him to be a pastor. He was studying to be a pastor through the pastoral track at Baptist Bible College in Springfield. Family and friends were in Denver, which made it even more appealing. They knew the area and saw the many needs and opportunities.

Haile Selassie, the last emperor in the three-thousand-year-old monarchy ruled Ethiopia for fifty years. He was born in 1892 to Ras

Mekonnen, who was a cousin to Emperor Menelik II. He became the 225th emperor of Ethiopia. He, along with many others, believed he was in the line of Menelik I, who was believed to be the child of King Solomon and Queen of Sheba. He took the name of Haile Selassie, which means "power of the Holy Trinity." Some foreign dignitaries attended his inauguration, which was a spectacular event among very poor people. In fact, some called him the "Conquering Lion." Around the clock, he was guarded by lions, cheetahs, and bodyguards followed by pet dogs. He constantly reminded his people that he considered himself elect of God. He placed himself as the sovereign of the nation and the leader of the Ethiopian Orthodox Church. With his administrative changes, there were improved civil services and a new tax system. There was a great undertaking for public works and road building.

In 1923, Haile Selassie convinced the League of Nations to accept Ethiopia as a member country. He hoped this would exempt them from the colonial ambitions of other countries. He toured through Europe asking them to help his country progress. It is said that everywhere he traveled throughout Europe, there were six lions, four zebras, and thirty attendants with him, which created a lasting impression among the other world leaders.

In 1934, Benito Mussolini, the dictator of Italy, moved against Ethiopia because of border issues with Somalia and Eritrea. As history is told, Haile Selassie went to the League of Nations to complain, but he did not receive much support, and Ethiopia was overtaken in April 1936. Haile Selassie went into exile. He entered Britain as a private guest after going to Jerusalem for a short time to pray. He continued to take his case before the League of Nations. He gave a very strong and challenging speech in June of 1936. Still they did not accept his plea, and they did nothing to help. Things began to change for Italy when they entered World War II as an enemy of Britain. Churchill secretly sent Haile Selassie secretly to Africa as

"Mr. Strong." In Khartoum, he began to organize his army of liberation, and in 1941, he returned to Addis Ababa. Ethiopia remained under the British until 1942 when they recognized Ethiopia as their own country. The emperor began to make advances for the people through education facilities. He enlisted other countries to help with developing Ethiopia. The Italians and Yugoslavians built dams and the United States constructed a new airport in the capital city. The Soviet Union helped with building educational facilities for higher education.

Ethiopia is a very mountainous region about twice the size of Texas. In 1960, there were around twenty-six million people made up of eighty different tribes. They were quite primitive and most lived in remote settings. The country did not have much of a road or rail system. There were very few health and social services. Most of the people lived in mud-walled and straw-roofed huts. More than 80 percent of the people lived more than thirty miles from any road. Each tribe basically had its own language, but the Amhara's tribal language, Amharic, was the official language spoken by nearly 50 percent of the people. Haile Selassie was of the Amhara tribe. Although Ethiopian Orthodox was the state religion, Islam was on the rise. There were also animists and Jews. Many believe the emperor wanted more missionaries to help slow the rising tide of Islam. The Coptic Church was large but not very evangelistic. Haile Selassie believed missionaries were going to be the ones to reach the people with the Gospel and help them with their educational and health needs too.

In 1959, a Sudan Interior Mission (SIM) missionary named Mr. Glen Cain contacted Dr. Fred Donnelson of the Baptist Bible Fellowship International (BBFI). Mr. Cain was Field Director for the SIM in Ethiopia. Dr. Donnelson was Mission Director of the BBFI. He told Dr. Donnelson that there was a great need for missionaries to go into the northern part of Ethiopia and that he was willing to help in any way he could to get the BBFI into Ethiopia. Dr. Donnelson had been a missionary in China for many years. Any prospect of a new field for missionaries was always exciting for him, and he immediately jumped at the opportunity to follow up on this request. He made a trip to Ethiopia, and Mr. Cain arranged for a meeting with Emperor Haile Selassie.

Mr. Cain had much experience in the diplomatic field, and he knew how to go about contacting the proper officials in the capital city and in each province. This usually took quite a bit of his time because application to meet with leaders took a while and had to be first be approved by several people. In 1960, Dr. Charles Billington and Dr. Donnelson had an audience with the emperor, Haile Selassie, after quite an effort by Mr. Cain. In her book *They Call Him Mr. Missions*, Mrs. Donnelson writes of this momentous opportunity. She shares the details of this important meeting from Dr. Donnelson's own journal.

As they arrived in the spacious ornate palace, they entered a beautiful hall with many decorations on both sides. At the end of the hall, the emperor was sitting on his throne. In front of him was a large globe. The emperor noticed Dr. Donnelson gazing at the globe, and he said, "Come, I too am interested in the world." It was customary to bow several times as one approached his throne, and Dr. Donnelson wrote: "I didn't mind bowing. I would walk on hands and knees all the way to obtain permission to give the Gospel to Northern Ethiopia." Several chairs were prepared before the throne. After being invited to sit, Dr. Donnelson presented his requests. He requested approval for the BBFI to do missionary work in Northern Ethiopia. The emperor agreed. He requested permission to build a student center near the university in the capital city, Addis Ababa. The emperor agreed and even gave a gift of property worth $30,000 near the main university. Dr. Donnelson also requested land and the ability to set up mission stations along the main roads to the north to do the necessary mission work. The emperor granted this request and said his government officials would work with Mr. Cain to make all this happen. Everything requested was granted! Then Dr. Donnelson promised the emperor one hundred missionaries during the next ten years. The emperor said, "These are pretty words. Now let us see some action!"

Within that week, they met with several crown princes and governors. They all wanted missionaries to come to their areas to the north to help their people. They knew what the SIM missionaries had done for the people in the south by elevating their conditions, educating their children, working to improve their health, and bringing spiritual hope to the people. Although these things were promised and approved, they didn't always go very smoothly. It took time to obtain land and permission for stations, even with letters from the crown princes and governors of the various areas. The Ethiopian Orthodox Church was an obstacle that oftentimes delayed opportunities. They even took Mr. Cain and the early missionaries to court, accusing them of harming the people.

Dr. Donnelson tells of one occurrence in court when the spokesman of the court finally responded for the three judges, saying, "You priests have been in control of your area for centuries, but you have done nothing for the betterment of the people. Wherever these missionaries have been, they have been a blessing to the people. Your priests have a Bible, and the missionaries have a Bible. It is identical. It is the Holy Bible in the Amharic language, the only Bible that is published in this country. Why should there be objection to their coming into your area and promoting the same Bible in which you believe?" Case closed.

Dr. Donnelson came back to the United States and began to plead for one hundred new missionaries. This was an exciting time in the BBFI. In a few months, he raised the money needed to build the large student center on the property given by the emperor. Though it was to be a student center to teach the students of the nearby university with a reading room and library, it also had nine apartments for the missionaries to use when they were back in the city. There would also be a large seven-hundred-seat auditorium for a church, plus classrooms for Sunday school.

Dr. Donnelson declared, "We need one hundred missionaries to go to Ethiopia right away. I promised them to the emperor of Ethiopia." Then he shared that it will not be an easy field, and missionaries were going to have to build their own homes, and they were going to have to live in whatever they built. Dr. Donnelson said we need several men who know something about building. Well, this spoke to Dad's heart. He thought about those who had to build the temple in the Old Testament in Israel. Even the building of that temple was the Lord's work. Well, he still had a year to go in school, and he was studying to be a pastor. It just seemed like this plea was constantly on his mind—the need for soul winners and church planters along with builders. It would truly be pioneer work in a new country where little was known and few had been. Finally, he had to speak with my mom about what was on his heart. Dad shared the idea of possibly going to Ethiopia as missionaries. Mom's response once again was without hesitation and to the point. She said, "That is okay with me. Whatever you believe God wants us to do, that is fine with me." She never opposed anything when it came to serving the Lord.

They decided to switch from the pastoral track of courses to the missionary track. Mom was then required to complete the missions program. Near the end of the year, my dad went to see Dr. Donnelson about being a missionary to Ethiopia. His first question was, "How old are you?"

Dad said, "I'm thirty years old."

"How many children do you have?" Dr. Donnelson asked.

"Well, we have three children."

"Oh. I'm sorry. You are too old, and because of your age, you will not be able to learn a foreign language."

For a moment, my dad was deeply disappointed. A thought came to his mind, and quickly Dad said, "I thought you wanted and needed builders to help the missionaries build their houses and build churches and school buildings as well as do the spiritual work?"

To which, Dr. Donnelson responded and asked, "Well, do you know how to do that kind of work?"

Dad said, "Yes, I have been a bricklayer for eleven years, and my dad was a contractor building houses, and I also helped him."

"Really?" Dr. Donnelson said now with great interest. "Okay, maybe you could learn a foreign language then."

That has been a discussion we have laughed a lot about through the years—especially since Dad has learned to speak two foreign languages. So they just took that as God's call, and that this was exactly where God wanted to send them as missionaries.

Dad finished his education, including the mission courses, and graduated in May of 1960. They moved back to Denver to do their internship under the leadership of Carl Boonstra. Ethiopia seemed to be the number one priority or interest of the BBFI at that time because it was a new field. Dr. Donnelson and pastors were very excited about what could be done there. Because of this enthusiasm to get missionaries to Ethiopia and the great zeal to get the Gospel there quickly, my parents were approved as BBFI missionaries in September 1960, after only six months of internship in a local church. They used to have multiple state BBFI meetings at the same time. Mom and Dad were approved in Castleberry Baptist Church in Fort Worth, Texas. D. A. Cavin was the pastor.

At the time of approval, the pastors asked Dad a few questions, but then Pastor Alvis Edmondson enthusiastically said, "Sounds like you have already been approved!" Everyone there laughed, and the process moved forward. Dad was qualified educationally, was of a more mature age, was a family man and a builder. All these things made it move quickly. While Mom and the kids drove back to Denver, Dr. Donnelson took Dad to another meeting in Jacksonville, Florida, to the BBFI meeting in Beaver Street Baptist Church to be promoted. Afterward, they flew up to Cincinnati to Landmark Baptist Church to be promoted in another BBFI meeting. They hit these three fellowship meetings all within one week. Those meetings were important, and most of them met at the same time. Churches immediately began, committing to support my parents. Dr. Donnelson paid for Dad's airfare all the way to Cincinnati. When he learned that Dr. Rawlings gave Dad a two-hundred-dollar-check, he told Dad that he could pay for his own flight back home to Denver.

They continued as interns at East Side Baptist Church in Denver until January 1961. As they did their internship, Dad's parents started attending East Side Baptist Church. They liked it a lot and attended regularly. The church was constructing a Sunday school building, and Dad, being a bricklayer, spent much of his time laying brick. His dad came over and laid brick with him on the building. My grandpa got to know Carl Boonstra and grew to appreciate him and listened intently as he would witness of God's love. Dad spoke often to Grandpa about God's love, and he always responded, "I have done too many bad things. It won't do any good." He continued to attend church and take his wife and two daughters. As time went on, Carl Boonstra kept visiting in their home, sharing what Jesus had done on the cross for them and all people. One evening, they all knelt at the couch in their home, and Carl led them all to Jesus Christ for salvation.

My mom's parents never opposed her going off to Ethiopia as a missionary. Her dad was a member of a Baptist church. Both sets of parents were always supportive of their kids being missionaries as God had called them.

It was not an easy time of raising support, even though it seemed like it was coming in quickly. They did not have much time to raise extra for personal belongings. They did what they could and saved where they could. Not many churches gave toward special personal needs. They had to purchase a four-year supply of clothes for the three kids because Ethiopia had very little to offer in the way of clothes and living needs. So they obtained five fifty-gallon barrels to be shipped that basically carried the clothes and shoes for the kids and a few other essentials. Mom had to figure out how much the kids would grow and how big their feet would become by a certain time during the next four years. They also built a 4 × 4 × 4 foot crate to hold other items, including one cedar chest and sent it ahead of them. Since they did not have much money, Dr. Donnelson had one of the groundskeepers of the Mission Office and Baptist Bible College make the crate that cost $75. These items would take nearly three months to get to Ethiopia's capital city going by sea on freighters. They would have to be unloaded and reloaded at many ports, changing from one freighter to another.

One time, my mom went to Dr. Donnelson and told him they did not have enough money for all the clothes and personal items needed. He said all the BBFI could do was loan them $100. They couldn't buy much with that, even back then. But they took it and made it work. Churches were mainly asked to support them monthly, but nothing was raised for equipment or personal needs. Karon Auterson was a student at Baptist Bible College at the time when my parents were getting all their things ready. She remembers Mom washing the clothes to make them look used so the customs officials would not charge for bringing in new items. She would sew name tags in each piece of clothing because the kids would be going to boarding school. Mom had heard that at the boarding school, they threw all the kid's clothes together to wash them and then sorted them out for the kids by the name tags. It was important to have their name tags sewn in them. Ole remembers rubbing his new tennis shoes on the concrete porch to make them look used before putting them in the barrel to ship them. You can imagine what Mom went through trying to guess how much the kids would grow each year and what the size of their feet would be.

Dr. Donnelson promoted my parents before churches everywhere he could, which helped them considerably in raising their monthly support. They moved back to Springfield so Mom could complete her required mission courses. She had three young kids at home, and Dad was visiting churches to raise their support as fast as he could. From the time they were approved until they left for Ethiopia in July of 1961, Dad was in eighty-nine churches to present the opportunities and needs in Ethiopia, as well as share their passion and burden for the people. Because of the enthusiasm for Ethiopia, the push by Dr. Donnelson, and the love for missions by the churches associated with the Baptist Bible Fellowship, the support came in from all over the country.

In those days, churches took them on for support for $5 and $10 a month. It was huge for a church to support missionaries at a level of $15 per month. That amount was good concerning the cost of living and the strength of the dollar. When they reached a promise of $500 a month of support, Dad stopped fundraising. Several churches would call and say they wanted to take them on for support, and Dad told them, "I have already raised the amount of support we need. You need to give that to another missionary raising their support."

One missionary wife, Margarete Vella, going to the Philippines with her husband, Joe, heard Dad tell this to a pastor, and she later told him, "I have never heard or seen a missionary turn down support." She couldn't believe it. High Street Baptist Church was one of the first churches to take them on for support as missionaries.

Not having a good car for deputation was a problem. The car they had when they drove to Springfield was a Chevy station wagon. The people at East Side Baptist Church in Denver said they needed a reliable car, and so they had the engine of the Chevy rebuilt. That engine and car lasted almost the entire time of deputation as Dad traveled from Baltimore to Los Angeles, from Key West, Florida, to Texas and all points in between. Dad can't remember how many miles he put on that car. When he finished visiting his last scheduled church and was coming home from the eastern part of America through Kansas, the car that had run so well for nearly eight months nonstop suddenly quit running just as he crossed the state line into Colorado. His dad came out with a chain and pulled the car the last ninety miles back home to Denver.

Mom was ready for an adventure as she looked forward to going to Ethiopia. Dad knew that God had called them, and now they were ready to make that move. Jacque thought it was neat to be able to go to Africa, and she was excited. What was ahead of them, they did not know. However, they knew what the Lord said in Matthew 28:18–20, stating that Jesus had all power, and He would be with them always. What a comfort that was, and what a promise to hold on to. It is a promise from the all-powerful, all-present, and all-knowing God.

CHAPTER FOUR

Buna – Coffee, Shy – Tea

My parents sold their small home in Denver that they were purchasing. After paying off the loan on it, they had some funds left over to buy clothes and other items, as well as pay for the shipping of the barrels and the crate carrying the cedar chest, ironing board, and a few personal items. There was also enough left to pay for their train tickets to New York and airplane tickets to Ethiopia.

Because they did not have enough to fly the entire way, they decided to take the train from Denver to New York. They carried their suitcases on the train with them. They did not have enough money to eat in the dining car, so every time the train stopped, Dad ran into the train station, bought candy bars and cookies, and then got back on the train before it took off again. When they arrived in New York, they stayed in a house that a lady rented cheaply to missionaries. They ate in the Japanese restaurant around the corner. While there for those few days of transition and waiting for their airplane, they got to see the Statue of Liberty and went up into the Empire State Building.

The airplanes in those days were propeller driven. Most of the planes for long flights had four propellers. They flew first from New York to London, England. After a few hours of layover in the airport, they flew from London to Rome, Italy. The kids took a lot of things to do on the plane. From there, they flew to Cairo, Egypt. In Cairo, they were not allowed to get off the plane until an official came and sprayed the plane with disinfectant to kill insects. Once that was over, they could enter the terminal for a short layover, and they were all given a glass of juice. Then they flew their last leg of the trip to Addis Ababa, the capital city of Ethiopia. It means "New Flower." Ole remembers landing in Addis Ababa in the propeller airplane. It was his first close view of Africa. While landing, they flew low over the huts, and he could see the people looking up at the plane. Seeing those people looking up and waving made a strong impression upon him. He thought to himself, "These are the people that we were coming to tell about Jesus."

It is amazing to think how the little girl who lived on Alcatraz, who grew up in Utah and Colorado, finally made it to Africa. Although she had a desire to be a missionary in China, she had no doubt that God had called them to Africa and specifically Ethiopia. It was going to be a life of adventure, and she couldn't wait to see how God was going to use them to hopefully bring many people to Jesus.

The first BBFI missionaries to arrive in Ethiopia were the Donahoes. They were waiting at the airport to welcome my family to their new country of service. Joel and Betty and their three children had arrived in Ethiopia five months earlier. They graduated from Baptist Bible College too and responded to the plea for missionaries to Ethiopia. They didn't get to Ethiopia right away, though. They were ready to leave soon after the appeal for missionaries, but because the BBFI was a new group going into Ethiopia, there were difficulties in getting entry permits. Even though the emperor had given the plea and permission, there was still a lot of government work to be done, and it didn't seem as though there was much hurry either. Because of this, Joel began to pastor a church in the Northeast of America and was having a lot of success with blessings from God. When the country finally opened, they immediately resigned the church and left for Ethiopia, arriving in February of 1961.

When my family arrived in Addis Ababa, they retrieved their luggage after an exhausting airplane journey across the Atlantic Ocean, through the continent of Europe, over the Mediterranean

Sea, and across Northern Africa into Ethiopia. It was July of 1961. Jacque was ten years old. Ole was nine, and Eric was four.

The BBFI had purchased a small vehicle that Mr. Cain used to do government work to enable the missionaries to enter the country. It could also be used by the other missionaries if they paid for the gas they used. The Donahoes used that car to go to the airport to meet my family. Joel told Dad that when they were planning to pick them up, they asked Mr. Cain for permission to use the car. Mr. Cain said, "You don't need to get them. They can find their way to the house." The entire family was so glad to see them waiting there, and it is no doubt very unlikely that they could have found their way to the house. They took everyone back to a house that Mr. Cain had rented in the St. Mary's district of Addis Ababa. It had two bedrooms, a living room, a dining room, and one bathroom. Mr. Cain's wife had passed away, and he moved himself to another location, so there was room for more families to live.

Mr. Cain was a huge help to those early missionaries. He had gone to Ethiopia as a missionary in 1928 when things were even more primitive, and he sure had some interesting stories that he could tell of those early days.

It had been such a long trip in propeller airplanes, and the family was happy to have finally arrived. Those planes really vibrated a lot. It was good to see somebody they knew, but everything was so new to them. Mom and Dad were very excited. They thought it was great that the house was right next door to the big tin building where they had church services. That was good for them to start right away getting with the Ethiopian people. The house was also on a busy street. They would go out on the street and invite people to church. My parents didn't know any of the language at first, but they had learned two sentences. When the people walked by them, they stopped and stared at Mom and Dad. My parents would tell them, "Come, enter." If the people responded by asking a question, they wouldn't know what was said. They just figured the people were asking why. The second prepared sentence was, "To hear the Word of God." Those were the only things they could say. Some people went into the church and then turned right around and came out. At least many of them heard the Word of God preached by Berhanu, the pastor at that time. They did see some people get saved while they lived there during those few months.

My parents didn't know where to buy anything, including food. They had a camping stove with propane gas for cooking. Mr. Cain told them they had to have somebody help them in the house. My parents had never had this kind of experience before. They hired a married couple. The man was to take care of the outside of the house, and his wife was to take care of the inside. They got a small salary, but they really were not needed. The place was small, and it seemed as if they were all getting in each other's way all day long. That couple ended up going with my family when they moved out into the countryside. They were a lot more useful and valuable there.

My family worked hard at learning more words to say. Some of the first words they learned to say were *buna*, which means "coffee," and *shy*, which means tea.

Mom was happy to finally be where God had called them to serve and minister. She had some anxiety taking three children to a new place without having much prior knowledge of the living conditions. She also dreaded the idea of her kids going away to boarding school. She knew it would happen and that it was necessary. She also knew Dad would work a lot to help get mission stations started with homes, schools, and churches built. This would all be new for her. However, she was ready for this journey and was ready to face whatever came her way, knowing God would watch over them while the people in the United States prayed for them. People in churches across America had given their word that they would pray. She wondered, would she be able to learn the language? Would her children be okay at school?

Where would they eventually settle, and what would they have to live in? Would the people be friendly and open to the Gospel message they were bringing? The new place they lived in upon arrival in Addis was not the best situation, but Mom knew she could make it work. She knew God had all the answers to her many questions.

Other missionaries arrived over the next months. Don and Laurie Brown came and lived in the same house in Addis for a while. Then Delmar and Helen Powell arrived. For a short time, several families all lived in the one house with the two bedrooms. At first, the Donahoes lived in it using both bedrooms for their family. They then moved to another town for language school, which made it possible for these new families to stay there.

A tin house was also built in the back of the property containing two rooms, with a verandah-type space between the two rooms. The two rooms were each ten by ten feet in size. The rooms had openings for doors and windows that were not yet in place. They were just open spaces. Those two rooms and verandah is where my family first lived. Next to the tin house was a mud house where the Ethiopian pastor lived. My family used the bathroom in the main house. There was an outside door directly to the bathroom that they could use. It really made for interesting living conditions for sure.

The beds and other furniture our family had were handmade from rough lumber. As time went by, they were eventually able to make windows and doors to fill in those open spaces. Any new missionaries who came ended up living in the main house. As others arrived, it got kind of crowded. That doesn't make for happy relationships, especially when you only have one bathroom.

During the time the Browns lived in the house in Addis, their room had a door into the only bathroom. The bathroom also had an outside door for my family to enter and use. The Browns or others would often forget to unlock the door when they were done using the facilities, and so a lot of times, my family couldn't get in to use it. They would often turn around and use the outhouse next to the pastor's mud house.

Ole was nine years of age when they arrived in Ethiopia. While playing outside in the small yard, he started thinking about his salvation. He was doubting his salvation. Negative thoughts kept coming to his mind. One day, he stopped playing and ran into the tin house and spoke with Mom about it. She said, "What was it that happened when you prayed to ask God to forgive you of your sins and save you?" He said, "Oh yeah. Okay." He went back out to play. Everything was settled.

Ole and Jacque went to Bingham Academy a few months after their arrival. That is what most missionaries did to educate their children. Bingham Academy was a missionary school with the SIM. Since the BBFI missionaries were associated with Mr. Cain, the children could go to school there as well if they wanted. This was not open to all missionary groups. There really wasn't much room for them in the two-room tin house the family lived in, so going to school and sleeping at the school was necessary.

My parents were learning to adjust to the culture, new language, and even the altitude. Addis Ababa is 8,100 feet above sea level. It is nestled at the foot of some mountains on a high plateau. The contrast between the old and the new was quite evident. The few modern buildings were surrounded by mud houses with tin or grass roofs. There were also a lot of ancient structures. They learned what food was available and basically how to live in this new place. The Donahoes were very helpful since they had already gone through this process. They became close friends. Soon the Donahoes moved to another town about an hour north called Debre Berhan. This is where the SIM also had a language school for their missionaries. If they had available space, they would allow our missionaries to learn there as well. My parents stayed in Addis Ababa trying to learn their way around. Mr. Cain continued going to the countryside looking for areas where mission stations could be set up with the idea of having elementary schools or clinics required by the government for our missionaries. If those things were done, then the missionary could do spiritual work. Mr. Cain worked hard at doing this, trying to find the right places in strategic areas where our missionaries could move.

The language school course was eight months long, and BBFI missionaries were only allowed to attend if there were no SIM missionaries who needed to go to the school. They had some houses at the language school all made from mud, which sounded terrible, but the walls were smooth inside and out. They were painted white. My family had one room in which to live. There was a common dining room for the families living there. Mom and Dad went to school in the mornings with their teacher. She was very good at teaching Amharic (Am-hair-ik). She was a nice single lady. The first task was to learn 200 sentences. These were common spoken sentences like greetings and certain questions. There are 256 letters in the Amharic alphabet. It is not an easy language to read or write and even speak. In the afternoons, my parents went on visitation so they could practice the language. They went into homes of the local people who were acquainted with the language school and happy to help. These locals knew why the students were visiting—to practice their language. They were always hospitable as they sat together while Mom and Dad used the sentences they learned. Then my parents had to listen carefully to the responses. For example, Dad would say, "What is this?" They would respond, "It is a chair." The students went to different homes every day to practice.

As with most places outside of the capital city, missionaries used out-houses for going to the restroom. The language school had several of them side by side. I heard a story of my brother Eric getting in trouble for throwing toilet paper rolls down the outhouse hole. There were some Ethiopian ladies assigned to watching the kids while their parents went to class. At times, they would be visiting with one another, and the kids could sneak off. Well, Eric had gotten away and went into one outhouse and threw several rolls of toilet paper down the hole. It looked like streamers flying down. Toilet paper was expensive and a special commodity. He eventually got caught by those ladies. I am not sure what my parents had to do to pay back the language school.

The ladies who watched the kids sometimes took them off the school grounds to a nearby forest where they would see baboons and other animals. That was always exciting. Once a year, the local Coptic Orthodox Church baptized their people at a special event. Many people gathered around the pool of water. Eric tried to get up close to the front to get sprayed as they performed their sprinkle baptism. He thought that was neat. The people had many beautiful umbrellas to protect them from the sun. It was an interesting, color-ful event.

My parents had been at the school nearly three months when they were told they would have to leave because one of their SIM missionaries was coming with a family and needed the spot in the classroom that my parents occupied.

The local pastor of the church located there had worked for Mr. Cain. He was asked to start teaching Amharic to my parents privately so that they could continue their learning. He started teaching them every weekday. However, Dad was also needed to start building a home for the Donahoes. He was not always in class, and Mom was there alone. One time, Mom corrected this pastor on the parts of speech in English. He got so mad at her because he was not used to women telling him what to do. He was so fuming mad he took off running down the street. Dad was there, and he ran after him. My dad was upset by the way the man acted. Dad chewed him out, and he never came back to teach them. My parents were new missionaries who did not always understand all the culture, and they sometimes made mistakes.

The student center in Addis Ababa was a building built by gifts from churches in the United States. Some churches such as Temple Baptist Church in Detroit pastored by Dr. G. B. Vick and Landmark Baptist Church pastored by Dr. John Rawlings gave large gifts. Many other churches gave smaller gifts. This building was promoted by Dr. Donnelson as a necessary thing, and it was. It was a priority for the BBFI to build.

Mr. Cain had a good relationship with the emperor. In their discussions, Emperor Haile Selassie gave the BBFI land near the main university. It was one and a half acres downtown and near government offices. It was a strategic place because it was near the university. This student center would be used to reach both the people in the area and the students.

Before the building was started, Mr. Cain took Dad to look at the property. They stood on the sidewalk looking over the fence around the property. There was a police headquarters nearby, and down below the property where the police had their mud houses where they lived. Mr. Cain knew the property had already been given. However, while they were looking at the land, some police officers came by and threatened to arrest them for looking over the fence. They said, "You are not allowed to look over that fence." They didn't know yet that it had been given to the BBFI. They said, "Don't ever look over there again." After a time of trying to explain it was now our land, the police finally let them go.

The idea for the building was that the first floor would consist of offices for the church, a library, and a few classrooms for students. The property started at the street level and dropped off quickly. That made it so that the first floor was on the street level, and there was one story below. It also had an auditorium going off to the back on the street level with seating for seven hundred. There were classrooms under the auditorium. There were three more floors above. Those floors above had three apartments on each floor for the missionaries who worked there or those visiting from the mission stations in the countryside. They would come to the city to visit their kids in boarding school, to get supplies, and to do other business and could stay in the apartments.

Denton and Jodi Collins were BBFI missionaries who led the church and managed the building. There was also a fenced-in place to park cars in the back. It was built by Mr. Senat Khalil, an Egyptian contractor. He and his family were believers and attended an SIM church. It was a stone building with a facade of little blue square tiles. Mr. Khalil even put his own personal money into it. This student center cost $150,000 in the early 1960s.

Denton Collins started a church there, and it was running approximately seven hundred. Other churches and Bible studies were being started around the city. God was blessing, and people were being saved. I remember times when our family stayed at the student center, and I saw students from the university in the building. They came to the library, and many of them heard the Gospel while studying in the building.

There have been discussions between our missionaries and other missionaries as to whether Emperor Haile Selassie was saved or not. He was known to be a Coptic Christian. Dad knew a man named Harry Adkins who was a missionary with the SIM in the southern part of Ethiopia. One time, Haile Selassie was in the town of Sodu

(Sow-dew) where the SIM was building some new buildings. The emperor went to see them. Harry was walking with Haile Selassie and asked him, "Your Highness, what are you depending on to get into heaven?" His answer was, "I am trusting in and depending on the shed blood of Jesus Christ." That was his testimony according to that SIM missionary.

Clarence Preshaw at guard tower on Alcatraz

Jeannine at Alcatraz - seventh from the right holding little purse

Parent's youth group with church deacon

Dad on deputation with Carl Boonstra

First headquarters in Addis Ababa

Dad in language school

First mission station in Robi

First Pioneer Unit in Robi

Mr. Cain and family

Our tent at Robi mission station

Dad with Sneeky Pete

Family by VW Pickup

Land owner in Kombolcha

Jon playing on sand pile

Building our Pioneer Unit

Our Pioneer Unit in front of our mountain

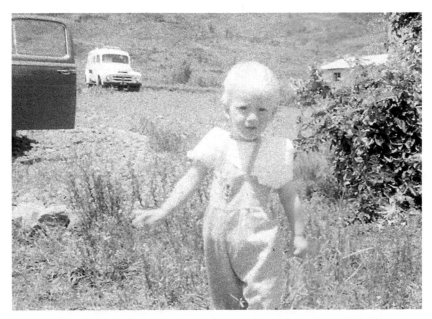

Jon with cast on

Dad with water project

Dad and Mom in front of our mountain

First church meeting in tent

Dad doctoring people

First Vacation Bible School in Kombolcha

Jon at Bati Market

Land Rover pulling cement mixer

CHAPTER FIVE

Two Years in a Tent

The Ethiopian government wanted all the BBFI missionaries to go toward the northern region. They required us to have schools to teach the children the basics of education. Dr. Donnelson agreed to this. At first, the missionaries didn't truly understand why they were requiring schools when they should be out preaching. It didn't take long to realize that most people could not read or write. If they were going to read the Bible, they were going to have to learn how to read. That put a different light on things, and the missionaries came to an understanding of the reasoning even though they had no training in running schools.

The decision was made to go north mostly along the main road toward the Red Sea. Along this main road, mission stations would be built in different towns to hold missionary housing, schools, and churches. The emperor's idea was that Christianity would combat the growth of Islam. Although missionaries of Islam had gone through the region decades before, the people were nominal in their faith and were basically Muslim in name only. However, they were not easily converted—as our missionaries would find out.

Robi (Roe-bee) was a small town with several villages in the lowlands after descending from the highlands of Ethiopia. It was at the base of a mountain range in which one would go down six thousand feet from the high plateau region to the hotter, more primitive region going north. There was a river that went through the town coming down from the mountains. To the north of the town were some villages and fields that the people plowed to grow their food. On the south side, there was a large forest. The temperature seemed to be hot most of the time. It was in Robi that our missionaries began the push northward with the Gospel. There were multiple tribes that lived in this area, and they were somewhat primitive. Mr. Cain did a lot of work in scouting out areas for mission stations. These were usually located where there were Muslim people because that's what the emperor wanted.

The first mission station in Robi had three acres of land that Mr. Cain acquired from the government. He always looked for signs of water when considering a location. He could tell by the plant life around the place if it had water for which to dig. He also liked to know if there was a river nearby. After obtaining this piece of land, they dug a well eight or ten feet deep. Water slowly began to seep in, and that's where they first got most of their drinking water, and they boiled it over an open fire. The property was on the edge of a forest, so there was plenty of dead trees and limbs for firewood.

When my family moved there, the first thing they had to do was clear out the tallgrass and cut down a lot of trees to make space for future houses, a school, and a church. There were two kinds of trees called acacia trees. One had yellow wood that was soft. The other was a red wood that was very hard. They didn't have power tools and had to cut everything by hand. They used axes to cut the wood. Mr. Cain had pipes welded onto the axe heads because the wooden handles broke too easily. Cutting all the trees down, plus cutting all the grass, was a terrible, tiresome job. The grass was nearly shoulder high.

On the south side of the mission station, the dense forest had a lot of tall trees and thick brush. To the kids, it looked more like a jungle. That forest is where the missionaries went hunting for meat to eat. There were a lot of wild pigs that ate grass and dug up roots to eat. You could track them by looking at places they were digging and eating. These pigs were very popular and tasty to eat. When my grandpa Preshaw (my mother's dad) came to visit, they took him hunting. One time, some of the missionaries went hunting, and Dad went off on a different path carrying a shotgun. He came to an open area and looked through the brush at something that moved. He saw a black leopard lying there. He got very quiet and tiptoed away backward. He told the others about it, and they all went to see it too, but it was gone. They often saw a lot of impala deer also.

Ole went hunting with Eric, and when they got near the river in the forest, they came upon a huge wild boar, and it scared them. The hogs would attack if they were startled or felt threatened. The boys quietly began to back up and walk through woods toward the station. Suddenly something was running through the bushes, and their hearts started beating fast. They just knew the pig was coming to kill them, and this was the end of their lives. Well, it wasn't the pig but instead a deer that came through the brush, and it ran right by them. Although frightened, they were completely relieved.

Once, Ole shot a vulture sitting way up high in a tree. He carried it home like a big prize, and he asked Mom if she would cook it for them to eat. Mom replied, "Get that thing away. Get it out of here! We don't eat those!" He asked if he could at least keep a feather, and she agreed.

The Donahoes and Richard Clark did a lot of hunting. Dad wasn't very interested in hunting, so he let them do it. They also hunted for guinea fowl. The men would go early in the morning and find them up in trees sitting on the branches. You could just aim your shotgun up into the trees and shoot a few at a time with one shot. This provided families with meat to eat.

Oh, you can imagine they had all kinds of hunting stories. The Autersons later came to Ethiopia. Frank loved to hunt and has so many stories to tell. One time, Richard Clark, another missionary who came soon after we arrived, was out hunting with the others. He wore thick glasses because of his poor eyesight. He took a separate path, and that led toward a ridge in order to look for wild pig.

Normally, he sat on a platform in a tree along a well-traveled pig trail, and he would shoot them when they came along. This time, walking along toward the tree platform, he was looking out ahead and stepped over what he thought was a tree trunk lying on the ground across the path. When he stepped over it, the thing moved. When he looked down at it, it wasn't a tree trunk, after all. It was a large python! Thankfully, it had the body of a deer in its mouth, and it left him alone.

The Donahoes were completing language school and beginning their move to Robi soon after my parents arrived in the country. Although my parents were starting language school, Mr. Cain needed help building a house where the Donahoes would live. Mr. Cain loaded up the walls for the pioneer unit on flatbed semitrucks. The truckers were willing to put these tin walls on top of their truckloads and transport them from the capital city to Robi. They unloaded them at the station and then continued to the coast with their main load. The walls weren't all that heavy because they were just studs of three by four rough lumber. So they cleared out a place for the first pioneer unit for the Donahoes. The units consisted of three rooms. Each room was ten by ten feet. That made the unit thirty feet long and ten feet wide. They nailed flat tin on the outside of the walls and then nailed boards like sheet rock on the inside. The units were built up on stilts, about two feet off the ground. This was so a person could crawl underneath and check for termites. The walls outside had corrugated tin four feet up, and then they put screen the rest of the way up because of the heat. A canvas was put near the top to be let down over the screen for privacy. It could be rolled up in the daytime. This would be a common preliminary house for most of the missionaries. It was something to get them set up quickly since there was very little housing available to rent out in the countryside. One room would be for a kitchen and storage room. One would be the living and dining room. The third room would be the bedroom. They built one room first and had it up on stilts so that the Donahoes could come and have a place to live. They came with their three children and moved into this ten by ten foot room. They had bunk beds made. It was a double wide bunk bed. Betty and Joel slept on the lower bed, and the three kids slept on the upper bed. They slept in sleeping bags in the one room and did the cooking and eating outside. These pioneer units also had wood floors. These floors came prepared along with walls. The kids called the pioneer units "PU huts." Later, as more missionaries came, they found mud-walled houses with dirt floors and tin roofs to rent. However, starting in Robi, there wasn't any other choice than these pioneer units. In the beginning, Mr. Cain and Joel helped Dad build these pioneer units.

After a few more missionaries had come and several pioneer units were built for them, they started to build the first cement-block house for the Donahoes. The BBFI was giving missionaries $10,000 to build or buy a house in every country the BBFI had missionaries. Then, for some reason, the BBFI decided to only give the missionaries in Ethiopia $5,000. That $5,000 was supposed to cover purchasing the land, paying the lease, or paying the rent. It was also to cover paying for the pioneer unit or for a permanent house.

In the early days in Robi, they bathed mainly by bucket with a washcloth. The missionaries may not have been the cleanest people. They dug a hole for an outhouse. The walls were made of corn shucks and plastered with mud. It had a tin room. In the first year, the outhouse collapsed into the hole three times. It only had a tree branch that you would sit on to do your business.

Joel had a dog. If someone left their house at night to go to the outhouse, about fifteen yards away, the dog would come out running after them. Many times, the person would get scared because they thought it was a wild animal, and they ran fast to get to the outhouse for safety.

Baboons came up from the forest on occasion to the mission station and near the houses. The Donahoe boys would throw rocks at them, and amazingly, the baboons threw rocks back. It sometimes ended up being a serious rock fight. Those baboons were mean, bold and had good aim.

When my family of five first moved to Robi, it was remote, and there were not enough pioneer units built. They bought an old used tent for $50. It was a nine by nine foot-square tent and did not have a floor. That is where they slept. They could hear the wild animals at night. At first, the ground was the floor; so when it would rain, they would get out of their cots in the morning and step right into the mud. Ole thought this was so wonderful. Later, the rains helped the grass to grow inside the tent. The kids thought it was great to have grass growing inside where they lived. They never experienced this in America. Later, they took one of the wood floors made for the pioneer units and put the tent on it. They didn't have much furniture. They acquired canvas cots that folded in a little bundle. They had three of those in the tent and two more for when Jacque and Ole came home from school to visit. They used pressure lanterns for light at nighttime.

They slept on those five cots at night and then took them down every morning so they could set up a table with a few stools to sit on. They also kept their camping stove and other valuables in the tent with them at night. Their first Christmas was spent in the tent. They received Christmas cards from family, friends, and churches. These cards were very special to them, reminding them of all those back in America praying for and thinking of them. Mom shared with me years later how she would sit in the tent and look at those cards. Not only did they bring color to the inside of the canvas tent, but they were a vivid reminder of the One they were serving. She remembered how helpful it was to see those cards and their messages of the Savior of the world. It was for the sake of Jesus that they sacrificed and lived the way they did so that people of Ethiopia could hear of His saving grace.

One of the valuables that Dad always kept in the tent was his manual typewriter. Dad was taught by Dr. Donnelson that missionaries should show respect and gratitude to the pastors and churches. He had a strong conviction that they should write to the churches, sharing their prayer requests and reporting of their ministry. He had to get a ribbon for it every time he went into the capital city so that he could do his monthly prayer letter. It wasn't that it was very valuable to the local people, but it was valuable to our family because that was how Dad not only reported to the churches but also kept in touch with the family. He would sit up at night in the tent, typing his letters under the light of a pressure lantern and swatting at mosquitos. Even though he hung the pressure lantern up about five yards away from the tent, the bugs were still around. He sent out seventy-five letters every month, individually typed. Dad typed using two fingers, plucking away at the keys.

Our parents never complained about the conditions in any way. Mom was adventurous and tried anything and was willing to live anywhere. Their attitude and trust in God made us feel secure and we knew that this life was God's will for us. We never questioned it.

Eric picked up the language faster than my parents because he played with the local kids all the time and learned it from them. One time, the prison warden who was a leader in the town approached Dad about a problem. Eric was there with Dad. A heated discussion occurred, and it scared Eric. Dad noticed Eric was scared, and he picked him up to hold him. Eric then called the warden a funny name he had learned from the local kids. The man started laughing, and the discussion calmed down. After that, the warden sent fruit over to our family for some time. Eric learned the language and spoke it as well as he spoke English. He played with the children as they watched over their goats. He enjoyed that so much that he wanted to become a shepherd himself.

Before digging the well for water, Mom and the other ladies walked half a mile down a dirt trail with tallgrass on both sides near the forest to the river. Certain times of the year, there was a lot of water, and other times, not very much. They gathered water into containers and carried them back to the mission station. It was always interesting whom or what you might see—men with spears, women and children getting water, cattle, goats, shepherds, and occasionally wild animals. There was always a concern of what wild animal, including snakes, might be in the tallgrass. This water was then boiled to be used to drink, wash the vegetables before eating them, and then to cook. This trip to the river would be made several times a day.

Many nights, Dad and Joel sat out by the open fire boiling a big pot of water for drinking and cooking. They talked about the ministry opportunities, the Scriptures, doctrine, and just how were they going to reach these people with the Gospel.

The place the well was dug was just outside of the mission station property. Since it was outside of the barbed-wire fence, the people began to use it too. The Danakils (Don-a-kills) came to water their animals there. Sometimes a calf would fall in, and they had to pull it out. That's where Mom and Betty started to get their water instead of the river. These tribal people were very primitive and didn't understand the concept of clean water. Later, Dad dug another well inside of the station and put a cement cap over it with a pipe and hand pump. This was to keep the water clean. In the meantime, they let people have the other well. It was up to them to keep it clean, but they usually didn't. It wasn't as important to them.

Mom had a one-burner camp stove on which she cooked. She cooked everything for the meal and then ran things back over the stove to warm them up just before eating. It was a long, drawn-out process.

She even learned how to bake a pie in a hole in the ground. It was an ordeal preparing meals. Usually, there was a group of people from the nearby village watching intently and occasionally laughing. The meat was either from wild animals shot out in the forest or purchased from wooden stalls during the market day. That meat from the market was usually not fresh. Most of the time, that meat had to be pressure-cooked for three to four hours before it was tender enough to eat. Vegetables and some fruit could be bought at the market a few miles back up the road in the town of Robi. There was a small market day on Wednesday and a large one on Saturday. My parents did not have a refrigerator and couldn't store their food for any length of time. It was a full-time job just to live and survive.

Once, the local veterinarian brought a dead porcupine as a gift to eat. To be courteous to him, the missionaries ate it. It had a unique taste and was greasy. But they ate it.

The Yarnells arrived in 1965. After a short time in language school, they moved to a small village called Jaraniro (Jah-rah-nee-roo). They were going to take over after the Powells left in 1966. Their mission station was off the main road up a couple of hills. The town on the main road near them was Kemise (Keh-mee-see). This town was farther north past Robi.

The people in that area were friendly. When the missionaries walked by foot or rode mules, the local people walked along and talked with them. The ones who had a Coptic Church background better understood the things of the Bible than the Muslims did. The Muslims would also listen when witnessed to and didn't get angry. The Yarnells went to many villages throughout the mountains. They built a school and church that met in the same building on their mission station. Children were the primary church attendees in the beginning, and then a few adults joined them.

Mules were more sure-footed for the mountain ministry than horses. If the local people couldn't handle or control their own mules, they brought them to the station and sold them to Lyle Yarnell. He grew up in the United States and had experience working with horses and mules for plowing. When he was six years old, he was plowing with four mules. As a little boy, he stayed out of his first year of school to herd the cattle and keep them out of his dad's crops.

One day, the wife of the crowned prince came to give land near Kemise so that Lyle could show the farmers how to plow using their mules. Lyle bought the equipment and collars and then taught the farmers how to plow with mules. They were very curious as they watched him handle the mules and plow the field.

Most of the farmers never could plow with the mules, so Lyle helped many grow crops by plowing their land for them. Rose Yarnell also rode the mules to town to teach children Bible lessons. It was about a forty-five-minute ride each way.

Like Dad, Lyle also had bricklaying experience before going to Ethiopia. He worked with Dad to build several houses and schools. He was a strong man and a hard worker. Lyle was a blessing to the missionaries. They truly lived off the land killing guinea fowl, warthogs, and deer. He would leave the house at six o'clock in the morning and return two hours later with something to cook and eat.

Once, he was standing with some of the young Ethiopian boys near their station. The boys started playing a game by jumping over a stick. They got higher each time. They asked him if he could do it, and he said, "No, if I do that, I will lose my teeth." They looked strangely at him. He jumped and pushed his dentures forward, and they fell to their knees, scared to death.

When Lyle would sit in his car in Addis, the poor kids would usually come along and beg for money or would just sit and stare at him. He would take his teeth out, and they would run away so fast. Lyle had heavy eyebrows, and when he looked at people for any length of time, they would get scared of him. They said he had this "evil eye."

The Yarnells also started a work in Kemise town. They rented a place with two rooms in a long-row building. It was made of straw and mud. Quite a few people came to that church. The place would be full, and the windows were opened. Muslims stood at the windows and listened to the preaching. People came from the surrounding villages too. Rose had vacation Bible school there with the kids. One day, the teacher/helper was beaten by the Coptic priest for helping the missionary. Most of the people were sorrowful and unhappy about that. They complained to the town leaders but the priest still continued to give problems.

Tefera was a tailor in Kemise town and had received Christ as his Savior. He invited many people to come and brought them to church. He had a sewing shop, so he knew many people. He helped bring many people to Christ.

Sarah and Sheba Yarnell went to Bingham Academy. Sarah was one year ahead of me. Sheba was three years behind me. They loved living in the country and really seemed to adapt well.

Mom and Dad moved north a couple of hours near a town called Kombolcha (Come-bowl-chuh) to start their mission station. The demand to build more houses increased because more missionaries kept coming and needed places to live. Eventually, several houses were built of cement blocks for some of these families in Robi. A few moved farther north to start new mission stations. They were the Powells, Browns, Autersons, Sidebottoms, Pierceys, Clarks, Metts, Vicks, Singletons, Wrights, Tyners, Hokansons, Bakers, Stampers, Morrows, Herrings, Worleys, Henrys, and the Lackeys.

During the first term, all cement work was done by hand. It was mixed on the ground using shovels. Past the city of Dessie in the mountains north of Kombolcha, the Lutheran mission station had a full-size cement mixer with a diesel engine on it. The missionary was willing to sell it. He asked $100 for it, which was a good price. Then he said to Dad, "Just give what you can." After thinking about it, Dad decided to give the fair amount of $100. He then built a trailer to carry it all around the countryside for his building projects. This helped speed things up considerably.

It became time to build the Donahoes a block house. They now had their four kids with them in Robi and were homeschooling them. The pioneer unit was getting too small. It was supposed to be temporary anyway. They needed a four-bedroom house.

Dad and several Ethiopians dug the foundation preparing for the stones to be laid. Several Ethiopians who could lay block were hired. As they started building the house, the rains started coming. It seemed every night it would rain, and all the water would flow toward the house and fill the basement hole. It would be two to three feet deep each time. Every morning, they had to bail it out with buckets, and this always gave them a late start on the building.

There was a nearby business run by Europeans in which they dried tobacco leaves. The missionaries got acquainted with them. They also sold stones carved out for building, and Dad bought some from them. It took weeks to put the blocks up around the basement area because of the rains. While working on this home, Dad also had to go back and forth to Kombolcha to complete our pioneer unit. He wanted to get Mom and Eric out of the tent.

Ababa and Amaday were working with Dad at that time, and they were a great help. They helped the hired masons with mixing the cement and bringing the blocks to them to be laid. Those two masons laid about fifty blocks a day. At that rate, it went very slow because they had to first do the stone basement, which was nine feet deep. Once that was completed, they poured the ring beam and started the block work for the walls above the basement. Something happened in the area with the tribal people, and the stone masons left out of fear. Dad never did know what happened, but he never saw them again. So Dad took on the work of laying the blocks. They were heavy and weighed close to forty pounds each. The two men mixed the mortar, and Dad laid an average of two hundred fifty blocks a day. Finally, they got the walls up and then built the A-frames with lumber brought on a truck from the capital city. The trucks carried the lumber on top of their own loads.

These truck drivers were Italian, and they always liked to stop in Robi and visit with the missionaries. They liked to play around with Eric. This influenced Eric to desire to be an "Italian truck driver" when he grew up. The drivers were always warning my parents to be careful letting Eric run around. They said there are big snakes in the forest all around, and they will swallow him up. They were serious about it. Eric thought it was great to watch those big Fiat trucks drive by with their large loads.

The A-frames were built. They were very large and heavy. They had to be lifted on top of the walls. Joel complained about this heavy work and about how it was quite dangerous. He often questioned out loud why he was up there. It was scary getting them up on top of the walls and walking them into place. Once they were put into place, the tin roof was nailed on. Then they put up the ceiling made of soft board. Interestingly, they put cornstalks on top of the ceiling and then put mud over them to be insulation from the heat.

All the flooring was made of cedar. That is all they had. It was tongue-and-groove flooring. There were a lot of delays waiting for the lumber and supplies to be delivered by the trucks. During those delays, Dad would leave to work on our pioneer unit.

Finally, they put the floor joists down made of two by six boards and the interior walls with 2 × 4s. Dad told Joel he was going for two weeks to finish up our own place. When he came back, all the floor joists and the wall studs had warped. The wood that had been delivered was not the proper wood Dad had ordered, and it was wet. The lumber company sent the wrong wood. They did not have much electric equipment or a generator. Dad mentioned this in a letter, and a man at our sending church sent a motor that was like an alternator in a car. Dad mounted it to the back end of the VW pickup near the engine. He ran the belt off the pulley of the engine to the alternator to get power. He ran his skill saw off it.

The Mission Office had promised tools like a table saw, drill, a generator, a truck, and many things needed to help, but Dad never got any of it. Dad just figured they were pioneer missionaries and would make it happen nonetheless. They took the studs and put a chalk line and cut the bow off and nailed it on the other side to make it somewhat square. They could not do much with the floor joists. This sure took a long time, and Joel got discouraged with all the delays. The living conditions were getting to him and his family, and he decided to take a furlough before the house was completed. Dad worked down there in Robi by himself a lot. He finally got our pioneer unit done in Kombolcha so Mom and Eric didn't have to go with him to Robi very much. They could now stay home. Dad took the tent with him and lived in it and ate what Mom made ahead of time for him when he returned to Robi.

Ministry work was unusual in that area because not only did they have the Amhara tribe and Muslims, but there was the Danakil tribe, who were nomads. They are herdsmen and followed the pasture lands into the Robi area and back to the desert.

The Danakil tribe wore very few clothes. The women wore a skirt from the waist down, and that was it. The men dressed the same way and maybe put a shawl over their shoulder. They mainly had cattle and sometimes a goat or a few sheep. Certain times of the year, they came up to where we were while the grass was green. They came into our area, and they would hang around while their animals were grazing in this forest. Joel tried to work with them. In fact, he learned the path they follow for a few days and tried to share the Gospel with them. Then they'd move to another area until the grass was all gone before they went back to the lowland. He would go out and try to work with them and teach them the Bible. The Danakil people were interested in us because there weren't a lot of white people around. They would come and sit and just watch us with great interest.

There was one warrior that Dad and Joel called Sneaky Pete. They called him that because all his teeth were filed to points and usually he would show up without making a noise. Many of the warriors did that as a sign of bravery. When he smiled, you could see them. After some time, he settled down and tried to farm on the edge of the forest. However, his own people attacked him and beat him because they didn't want him to be a farmer. They believed he should only be a nomad. Dad got to know Sneaky Pete well.

One day, Sneaky Pete came into the main house that Dad was building for the Donahoes, and Dad noticed something was bothering him. He got in Dad's way while he was standing up on a stool hammering nails into the ceiling. My dad playfully acted like he was going to hit Sneaky Pete on the head. Oh, Sneaky Pete got very mad and started saying, "What is it, what is it?" Dad got off the stool, and they stood there nose to nose just staring at each other. Dad was ready because he was not sure what Sneaky Pete might do. He might pull out a knife or something. Well, he walked away. He came back a few days later. You had to be careful if you acted like you were joking or playing because they did not understand this and would take it seriously. Sneaky Pete became friends with the missionaries, and they would often see him around as he continued to be a farmer.

As far as witnessing to people and seeing them trust in the Lord, the missionaries didn't have many results among the nomadic people. Those people didn't understand what the missionaries were talking about. They claimed they were Muslims but didn't know anything about that either. The emperor had asked our missionaries to work with and reach the Muslims. They were not fanatical. Most of them were not educated and couldn't read or write. They only knew the little of what the Imams had taught them. The Muslims in that area claimed that God has one hundred names. Human beings know ninety-nine of those names, and only the camel knows the one hundredth name. They say that's why the camel always has a smile on its face.

The Danakil tribe were fighters. At certain times of the year, they came up from the remote desert areas. They came looking to get married. For them to get married, they had to kill a man from another tribe. During those times, the local people would tell the missionaries because they were now friends, "Don't let your boys go into the forest. They must stay inside the mission station and not go into the forest." You see, a Danakil of the age to get married had to kill a male of another tribe and cut off the testicles and give them to the bride-to-be. She would wear them in a pouch around her waist. This proved the man was worthy of the father's daughter. Dad told Ole and Eric when it was not a good time to go hunting because he said, "It was mating season." They weren't sure what that meant exactly, but they obeyed. Dad told them it would be a great prize for the Danakil to get one of them. They never went out of the station when he said not to do so.

One day, when Ole was a little older, he was hunting with a few missionaries and somehow got separated from the group. They were trying to track down some wild pigs and guinea fowl. Suddenly, Ole was surrounded by a band of warriors. It was a nervous time for a moment. Ole was hoping none of those warriors were getting married and needed to kill him to prove they were worthy for a man's daughter. Since he was white, they let him go. For many of them, it was the first time to see a white person.

They also did not usually confront a person face-to-face when they had a problem between them. Everyone had rifles left over from the Italian war. Some of the guns didn't work, but they looked tough and mean, and you didn't know if they worked or not. They would walk along a trail with the one they had a problem with as if there were no issues. They would carry their gun over their shoulders and pointed at the guy they were walking with and then pull the trigger with the gun aimed at the other guy's head. One time, Joel Donihoe heard somebody get shot, and he ran to see what was going on. When he got there, he found that several Danakil warriors had killed a man, cut him open, and they were then eating his liver. They said he was brave in the way he fought against them. They believed if they ate his liver, it would make them brave too.

There were also people in the area from the Amhara (Ahm-hah-rah) tribe. They were a little more civilized and were farmers or had small businesses in town. They were the ones that would eventually come to the church services once they were started. At first, there were a lot of children who came to the services. Some of these children grew up to be Sunday school teachers and learned to reach their own people with the Gospel.

The Autersons and the Sidebottoms eventually had horses and mules. They would ride them through the mountainsides to the remote villages in order to teach people how to read and write and then teach them Bible stories. A few people would believe, but mostly it was the children who did.

Karon Auterson was a nurse, and she would often be seen helping people with various wounds and ailments. She became very popular in the area. I liked Mrs. Auterson a lot. She would hold me and count my ribs and tickle me. I would laugh and laugh so much. I enjoyed walking with her at the market too.

In those days, the Danakil people were primitive in many ways. One day, Dad was working by himself on the tin school building near a hill on the edge of the station. It was market day when the people would sell eggs, chickens, goats, vegetables, and various other foods. Richard Clark had hired a man to watch the station in the daytime. There was no fence around the station at that time, so people oftentimes rode their mules through the station. Richard had a large garden, and they would just walk or ride right through it, so he hired a young man to protect the garden and station. This young man had poor eyesight.

On that particular market day, a man came riding on his mule and rode right through the garden. He was someone important because he had four men running along behind him. When the guard chased after him and told him he was not supposed to be on this station and ride through the garden, the four men gathered around him ready to beat on him. Other people saw them and came and joined in by yelling at the young guard. So the young man started making a strange trilling noise often made when in time of danger. The Danakils didn't think twice about killing someone, and they were ready to take this young man's life. Dad left the building and ran over there among the big group now gathered near the hill. It was about forty yards away. They circled around him, and the guy kept making that noise. The people saw Dad coming and opened a pathway for Dad to walk through. Dad grabbed the young man by the nape of the neck and carried him out. The people quieted down and just watched as they both walked away. Amazingly, they left both alone. It was kind of scary for Dad, but he wanted to help this young man and took the chance that nothing would happen to Dad, either.

CHAPTER SIX

Once Every Three Months

Whenever I mention boarding school to someone, I usually get a response of sympathy. Most do not know what boarding school is and think of it more like a detention center, a place for bad kids or a place where parents send their kids when they don't want them around.

Back in the '60s and '70s, boarding school was the method that many missionaries utilized for their children to get the education they needed, especially in Africa. There were very few homeschooling options then. Some missionaries with the BBFI tried homeschooling on their own, and some succeeded. But in those early years, it was much harder. It took both parents teaching every morning until noon. This was not easy to do along with ministry and just trying to live in the difficult conditions in Ethiopia.

Our family situation made it challenging for us to homeschool. We were first living in a tent in a remote area, and it took most of Mom's efforts just to live. Even cooking the food took a lot of her time. Then you think about Dad always being gone helping other missionaries with their building projects. So my parents sent the two oldest ones to boarding school. When Eric was six years old, he also went for the first grade. When I was ready for first grade, Jacque was in the eleventh, Ole the tenth, and Eric the fifth grade. It would have been impossible for my mom to teach all of us with that range of ages and grades while Dad was often gone. Plus, trying to do ministry at the same time would have been hard. We just thought this was part of pioneer missions. There wasn't any other choice for the most part for our family.

Jacque and Ole went to boarding school a few months after arriving in Ethiopia. They went to school at Bingham Academy, the boarding school under the Sudan Interior Mission (SIM). The SIM was willing to let our BBFI kids go to school there because of our connection with Mr. Cain. All the SIM children went to school there. Bingham had one big main building. There were also some buildings for a dining room, several dorms, and classrooms. There was a huge swing set. Those swings could go very high.

Jacque was in the fourth grade, and Ole was in the third grade when they started. If we were in town, they could get out on the weekends, which usually occurred once every three months. The only vacations for which they could come home were summer and Christmas. The rest of the time they were in boarding school. It was not easy for my parents to be separated from their kids. My parents didn't cry when they left us until they got down the road a way, and then they started crying. They thought at the time if the kids didn't see them crying, the kids would not cry, but it wasn't true. Ole would go off behind one of the buildings and cry. Jacque seemed to do okay. Our mom usually cried most of the twelve-hour drive home. Mom and Dad were told not to visit the kids too much because it would only make it harder on them. My dad now admits after looking back that it was not good advice.

On occasion, we got to ride in a DC-3 propeller airplane to go home. It could barely clear the trees on the tall mountains because of the high elevation. Then when we approached Kombolcha, the plane would circle the airfield until the people got their cows off the dirt airstrip. The pilots were usually American pilots. Sometimes they let Jacque sit up in the flight deck. They would ask her if she wanted to fly the plane, but she was always too afraid. Most of the time, they had wooden benches down the sides to sit on. Small animals like sheep and goats and chickens also made the trip with us. There were no seat belts.

Eric begged my parents to let him go to be with Jacque and Ole at boarding school. He didn't completely understand what it would be like to leave his parents for an extended amount of time. He was always excited when his siblings came home, even though Ole, his older brother, was tough on him. Eric still missed them and was happy to see them when he could.

When Jacque and Ole came home for summer and Christmas breaks, Eric and I always begged Ole to play with us. After a while, he'd get tired of doing that, and Mom would make him keep playing with us. One of our favorite things to play was cowboys and Indians with our little plastic men and forts. Well, Ole had had enough. He obeyed Mom to play with us again. He told us, though, that this time it was going to be for real. Man, we got excited. Ole really got animated about it with us and told us to build our forts, put grass around them, and have our men all inside ready to fight. He brought his Indians and placed them strategically around the forts in the grass. He asked if we were ready because it was going to be for real. Oh boy, were we ready! He got out matches and started throwing them at the fort and grass as if the Indians were shooting arrows with fire tips. It was amazing, exciting, and so real! Things caught on fire, the fort began to melt, the men melted, and when it was all done, it was all just a mess of plastic that could never be played with again. His plan was successful. He never had to play that with us anymore.

We could visit them at school if we drove two hundred miles from Kombolcha to Addis. Those two hundred miles took twelve hours or longer to drive. When we got to town, we only got to see them for fifteen to thirty minutes. Our time was limited because of all the things that needed to be done while in the city and because Dad felt he needed to get back home for the work. The kids basically lived and grew up at school. Bingham Academy only went through the ninth grade, so when Ole and Jacque were too old to attend there, they went to another mission school called Good Shepherd School. This is where Jacque finished her high school years and Ole through the eleventh grade.

Ole felt he had to go to boarding school so that Dad could do what God called him to do. As difficult as it was, he just felt that is what they were supposed to do. He was neither against it nor loved it, but he always understood why they went away to school. As a nine-year-old boy at school, he saw God answer his prayers. One time, Jacque lost her ring when playing volleyball, and she really liked that ring. When she lost it, everyone looked for a while, but they didn't find it. Eventually they quit looking, and they all left. But Ole stayed there and prayed. He knew it meant a lot to her. He prayed and believed God put into his mind to get a broom and sweep on the cement where there was some sawdust. Then he threw the sawdust in the air, thinking if it was there, it would fall and make a noise when it landed. He did this several times, and suddenly he heard a noise like a ring on the cement. He was so excited and thanked God and took it to Jacque.

Ole lost some money once, and he couldn't remember where he had put it. He laid on his bottom bunk bed and started praying. He shared with God how he needed this money. After praying, he opened his eyes, and there the money was in the springs of the bunk above. He never remembered putting the money there.

When Ole and Jacque first went to Bingham, the dorm parents and teachers were all with the SIM. It was their school for their kids. That school was initially in America on the east coast. The SIM missionaries left their children in America for four years until they returned on furlough. As you can imagine, this was extremely hard on the families. Therefore, they moved the school to Ethiopia closer to the missionaries. They assigned missionaries to the school as teachers, dorm parents, and administrators. That is not why most of them went to the mission field. They went as missionaries to evangelize, to start churches and other kinds of ministries. They did not agree to go to Africa to work in a school. So sometimes they would get frustrated and take it out on the students. In the early years, their frustration kind of got out of hand.

If the boys high-jumped without shoes, the dorm parents beat the bottoms of their feet. If they made a salt ball in the dining hall with salt and water during mealtimes, they had to drink a full glass of salt and pepper in water before going to bed. They finally changed it so there had to be another adult as a witness to the judgment.

They did not treat the kids as good dorm parents, console them or give them the attention they needed. Ole remembers it seemed like everyone was always doing wrong. It affected many of the kids who later in life had to deal with many issues.

The dormitory building's walls were made with mud plaster over them. The plaster had been painted. In the hallway between the boy's rooms were pictures of airplanes on the walls. The boys had made bows and arrows from the tree branches in the forest nearby. Some boys thought it was cool to shoot their arrows at those pictures as if trying to shoot down the planes. The arrows stuck nicely into those mud-plastered walls. Ole walked in and thought this was the greatest thing he had ever seen. There was only one problem. He didn't have a bow and arrows, and he never got a chance to shoot any arrows. So he found the next best thing. He found a hatchet and started throwing that at the planes and sticking it in the wall. The dorm parent came in and caught them and said they were all going to get a spanking.

All the boys lined up to get a spanking from the dorm parent. It finally came to be Ole's turn, and the dorm parent asked if he was shooting arrows into the walls. He said, "No, I didn't have any, but I was throwing a hatchet at them." The dorm parent said, "Go on, I am only spanking those who shot arrows." I can only think of the worse damage the hatchet was doing, and yet he got off free.

They got a lot of spankings for getting into trouble. The older boys would chase the younger boys and hang them upside in the trees. When they were chasing Ole, he started crying, especially after catching him. They finally let him go. He went to his room and prayed for his buddies to be released from the trees. Ole remembers that sometimes the older boys would take rocks and carve their initials in the foreheads or arms of the younger guys.

They went into the woods on the lower part of the school campus to shoot pigeons with slingshots. They made little fires and cooked them. They took potatoes from the storage area and put them with the coals of the fire to warm up. They cooked the meat until it was black just to make sure it was completely cooked. The meat was cooked so long that they could even eat the bones. The potatoes were black from the coals and fire. When they returned to the dorm, they had black soot all around their mouths. The dorm mom asked where they had been. They answered "nowhere," not knowing black soot was on their mouths. They got spankings for that.

Ole remembers they would wake up in the morning and have flea bites all over them. But for some reason, Ole never had any bites.

If it weren't for sports, boarding school would have been a lot harder for Ole. He loved to run in races and play every sport. When he and Jacque got rheumatic fever, the school made them stay in bed two months. They couldn't go to the dining hall, and Ole couldn't see his girlfriend. He made a telescope to look out of his dorm window. He sent a message to her to stand at a certain place at a certain time so he could look out at her. They couldn't go to class and had to do their homework in bed. Well, after that episode with the fever, he didn't have the wind to run like he used to.

One of the good things about the school was learning all the memory verses. Ole was good at it. In the tenth grade, they had to say 150 verses with the references and the subjects at one sitting. Ken Isaacs was the smart one in Ole's class. Ken asked if he could say the verses without the references and subjects. They approved his request. Ole went ahead and said them all with the references and subjects, never realizing that one day he would be a preacher.

One girl named Marilyn learned 1,500 verses and quoted them in one sitting. The teachers listened for three hours. They would take turns listening to give each other a break while the other continued to listen.

The Gihon (Ghee-on) was a hotel and restaurant that had a swimming pool. The water was filthy and dark. Most of the time, you couldn't even see the bottom on the deep end. Once they found someone dead on the bottom! Bingham took us there for an occasional activity, sometimes as a reward for quoting many memory verses. It was fun to swim there.

Jacque learned to play the piano at Bingham. She had good teachers for that.

A few years later, Eric went to school at Bingham. He ended up having a tough time being left by Mom and Dad. He was close to Mom and usually followed Dad everywhere he went when building. Being away from them was hard. In fact, when they would leave him behind and drive out of the gate of the school, Eric would chase the car as they left him behind. The main guard, Kasa, would chase after Eric to stop him from leaving the campus. You can imagine how hard this was on Mom and Dad. I know they were crying too, but they waited until the kids could not see them.

The school had washing machines that had roller wringers on them. You took the clothes out and then put them through these two rollers, which squeezed the water out of them. One day, Eric had an accident in his pants and was afraid of getting into trouble. So he washed them himself and then he decided to get them wrung out. He put his clothes into the rollers. They got a little crooked, so he tried to straighten them out. But his hand got caught, and the rollers pulled his hand through up to his elbow. He started screaming. Jacque heard it, and she knew it was his scream and ran to help. He was okay but really scared. Jacque felt like a mom to Eric at school. Eric slept in his dorm room on the lower level floor, and Jacque was on the upper level floor. Most nights, Eric would go to the bottom of stairs and cry and call for Jacque. She would get him and take him to bed with her.

The school had services on Sunday afternoons called LAC. It stood for Loyal Ambassadors for Christ. They had special music, and some of the students participated. We had our offerings to give that our dorm parents gave us. It was the same coin every time, and they would take that offering from our parent's account. Someone would preach and challenge us from the Bible. Then on several occasions throughout the year, they had special school performances, from plays to musicals.

Usually, the kids were kept busy in the day and lonely at night. It was not easy for them. Once a year, they allowed the kids to raid the kitchen to a degree. The students all ran to get sweetened condensed milk. They put it in a pan and boiled it until it came out as caramel.

When I went to Bingham, things had changed for the better. The dorm parents for the young boys believed God had called them there for that purpose—to be dorm parents to the boarding missionary kids. This made things much better for us than it was for Jacque and Ole. I knew the dorm parents cared for me, and they consoled me when I missed my parents. They helped me with homework. They allowed us into their apartment as if it were our home too. Even though they had their own kids, they loved us too.

I built good friendships with the other boys my age. When we missed our parents, the friends would come help to console each other. We all had our bad days, and we cheered each other up.

Oh, we had fun at school too. At night, they had story time. We were all in our pajamas ready for bed, and we loved to hear the stories in the dorm parents' living room. They read stories like *Pilgrim's Progress*. Then sometimes, after we went to bed, we would dare each other to run to the bathroom after lights out and see if you could make it there and back without getting caught. There were multiple rooms with about six to eight boys in a room. We could hear other rooms running, and so we would join in. You had to pump yourself up because this was pretty scary. To be able to get there and back without getting caught was a huge achievement. Well, one time my turn came. I got out of bed, stood at the back of the room, got up my nerve to go, and took off. I was going to make this a quick trip— faster than any of the others. When I got to the door, my speed was pretty good. I adjusted for the left turn I had to make, knowing that a few steps later, I would turn right into the bathroom. As soon as I got to the door, the dorm mom stepped out. She was a pretty good-sized lady. I ran right into her. It totally stunned me. We all got in trouble that night, and everyone got a spanking. Another time, we got caught horsing around, so the next morning, we had to run laps around the soccer field until breakfast.

Oh yes, we would get sick every now and then. Usually we were not truly sick, but we knew that when we were sick, we could get a mint if we had to stay in bed all day. Man, that was worth it. Of course, you had to time it so that it didn't seem like you were getting sick very often, or they would catch on to you.

When our parents would leave us at school, they left us with a box of candy. Every kid had their own "candy box" that the dorm parents kept. On Saturdays, we could go to our box and take two to three candies out. There were certain candies in Ethiopia that were hard and in green-and-gold wrappers. They were amazing! They were narrow and long and had the best taste. These were popular for trading. This is probably where I learned to be a good negotiator because we would trade candies with each other, and some were more "valuable" than others—in our opinions.

Every morning we got up at six and, in our pajamas, headed off to a classroom to memorize verses. We would memorize certain verses or sometimes whole passages that were assigned to us. I am not sure how many verses I memorized through the years, but I am sure it is in the hundreds. Even today, I can recall some of those verses because of memorizing them back in grade school. If you memorized a certain number each semester or year, you got certain awards. One year, I memorized the maximum and achieved the highest reward. They took those of us who accomplished this feat out to the airport to eat at a restaurant and show us around the airport. That was the coolest thing ever!

We ate at assigned tables. Usually, the tables ended up having races to see who could finish and get out first. The older kids were the table leaders and made the little ones cram the food down. You couldn't leave until everyone at the table was done eating. Sometimes, the older kids didn't like certain foods, and they put it on the younger kids' plates. That happened to me with cooked carrots. To this day, I can't eat them at all.

Below the dorms was a small forest. It seemed big back then. It had a huge swing called the "bag swing." It was tied with chains to tall eucalyptus trees. We could swing very high on that. The school built a ladder platform to pull the swing up higher, and then we could jump on the swing and go way out. It was amazing. You could ride from tree to tree high above the ground. At some points, you could be thirty feet or higher off the ground. It could be a little dangerous. Some broke their arms hitting the trees wrong, going too fast or falling off. Ole and John Flynn were in the third grade and were taking turns on the bag swing. Ole watched John swing way out, and he suddenly fell off from very high up in the air. Ole thought he must be dead. When he got to where John landed, it was in the middle of some trees next to a pile of stones. John had landed in a place with soft dirt and missed all the danger. Ole asked if he was okay, and John said, "I think so." From that point on, they believed that God had something very special for them to do because John did not get hurt. So the boys decided they would start preaching. They would get the first through third-grade boys together and preach to them. They visited them like a pastor would, all in the hopes that they would get saved. John and Ole did that for about six months.

We oftentimes went down into that forest and had acorn fights. On Fridays, we loaded up our supplies of acorns and rocks and headed down to the lowest part of the campus near the fence. On the other side of the fence was a river, and on the other side of the river was a field that was part of a school for Ethiopian kids. We gathered on our side of the fence, and the Ethiopian kids gathered in that field on their side of the river. We had serious acorn and rock fights. Some of us even made slingshots to use. They usually hit us a lot more than we hit them. On some days, it got quite intense. I don't think that is what the school had in mind for us, and it certainly was not the way of reaching out to the community.

Sometimes there were protests or riots in the city. The section of the city that the school was in was not the best. The school grounds did have a tall corrugated tin wall all the way around except along the river. I don't remember feeling afraid or threatened by the riots. However, there were times when we were made aware of the possible dangers that were out there. I am not sure how often, but we had safety drills. We had places for our respective classes to go when the siren went off. The school had some tunnels and rooms under some of the buildings, and we went to those safe zones. They had stockpiles of food and supplies there in case those events would go on for days. In my years there, we never had to use them for real, only in drills.

The situation for Jacque and Ole became interesting since Bingham only went through ninth grade. They had to go to Good Shepherd School for their junior and senior years. They got permission to sleep at Bingham, and every day they rode a van across town to Good Shepherd School. Later, Dad bought Ole a motorbike for their transportation. As they drove to school, sometimes kids threw rocks at them. One time, a kid hit them, and Ole slammed on the brakes. He left Jacque with the bike and ran after the kid. He chased him all the way to the boy's hut and ran in after him. It was pitch-black inside. When Ole's eyes adjusted, he noticed about fifteen women sitting inside. The boy was screaming, and the mother handed the boy over to Ole. He figured he had been frightened enough and gave him back to his mom, and they went on to school.

Often I would wait at the gate for them to come back to Bingham just to see them. Jacque was like a mother and often consoled me. One year, they lived with the Sidebottom family in Addis. Jacque shared a room with Rhonda. Ole, Dennis, and Michael shared the other bedroom. Jacque graduated from Good Shepherd School in 1970.

Field day was a big occasion at Bingham Academy. Every child from every grade participated. The parents were usually on hand to watch these events and cheered for their kids. They had many track-and-field contests from racing and high jumping to discus throwing. Throwing the discus was Ole's sport. Once he threw it, and the discus flew through an open car window. He got in trouble for that even though it was an accident. In one competition, he threw it, and the discus hit telephone wires going across the field overhead on his first throw. The second throw was not bad, but not his best. The third and last throw went so far and good that he ran after it to see the distance. He was disqualified because he stepped over the line before it was done moving. Ole enjoyed the pole vault and landing in sawdust. He liked a particular relay, and he was always the person on the last leg. The person on the last leg of the relay had to eat a loaf of bread and then whistle to finish the race. Both the girls and boys competed. There were three-legged and potato sack races too. They had ribbons for first, second, and third places. I remember going to watch Jacque, Ole, and Eric compete. Eric was a fast runner and usually won the races with the boys his age. I remember hearing one boy say, "Oh no, Eric is in the race. There is no use running." The boy's dad told him, "There is still second place to run for." Jacque appreciated her two brothers sharing their ribbons with her for the pictures that were taken. At least in the pictures, it looked like she had won some ribbons. It was a very festive event for the school, the parents, and for the missionary kids.

Our parents visited us once every three months. Mom bought us presents when they came because she missed us so much and felt bad that we were away from them. She often did without things she needed so that we could have things. My favorite food is cinnamon rolls. When they came to visit, she always brought me cinnamon rolls. Sometimes, she sent some with other missionaries coming into town. She made the best cinnamon rolls. When they did come to Addis for supplies of food and building materials, they usually only had about fifteen minutes to visit us. That was fifteen minutes a day for three to four days. Also, the school kept us so busy that our schedules did not always make it convenient for spending time with our parents. Our dorm parents had us write letters every week to our parents. Mom wrote us letters about as often. Those letters are what kept me going and knowing that Mom missed me and prayed for me.

For half of fifth and all of sixth and seventh grades, I went to Good Shepherd School. Mom and Dad moved to Addis for a year and a half, so we went to that school since it allowed day students. I boarded there in seventh grade. Although Mom never complained of being alone, the living conditions, her health battles, or about being a missionary, she still struggled with two things. The first struggle was having to send her children to boarding school. She was like any other caring mother. It was not easy to send your kids a twelve-hour's drive away from home to school. She knew it was the way it was done in those days and in a country like Ethiopia. My parents did the best they could with this situation. They were always very positive about it and never complained in front of us. Mom usually had one child at home, however, sending off a six-year-old child to school was not easy, considering she might only get to see them once every three months.

Her second struggle was she thought she was overweight and would get depressed over that. One of the doctors in Dessi (Deh-see) wanted to help her, and so he put her on dietary medicine to which she became addicted. Because of this, Dad felt we needed to be in the city closer to the school for Eric, who was having a difficult time and in town to be more available for Mom.

In the mornings, Dad drove me to school in a blue Fiat 850 at Good Shepherd School. Later, Dad bought Eric a motorcycle. It was a Suzuki 185, and Eric drove us to school every day. Eric was a good rider. Once we were going down a small hill, and a car came in our lane. To avoid that car, we had to leave the road and hit the little hill. We went airborne about seven feet off the ground, and I held on to Eric for dear life. The back wheel was higher in the air than the front wheel. However, Eric landed in the small place that was only wide enough for us, and he kept the bike upright. I was shaking and amazed we were not hurt at all. On another occasion, I got hit in the leg by a taxi, but we just kept going, and I was okay.

I enjoyed playing basketball and running cross-country at Good Shepherd School. With Addis being at such a high altitude, running the long distances was hard. However, I was good at it. Can you imagine running against Ethiopians in long-distance races? They were good then and even better today.

We were not angry at our parents for leaving us at boarding school. We felt like they gave us a choice: to be with other kids at school or learn at home. We mostly just wanted to be with other kids, play sports, and learn to play instruments like the piano. As a girl, Jacque was limited in what she could do in the countryside, as far as playing with the local village kids. She preferred being with other missionary kids at boarding school.

While Dad was gone most of the time helping other missionaries with their buildings, Mom was left at home in the countryside. This was a lonely time for her, and she would dwell on her kids wondering how they were doing. Were they crying? Were they hurt? Were they sleeping at night? Were they learning? Were they struggling in any way? So many things would run through her mind about each one of the kids.

This began to weigh heavily on her mentally and emotionally. Not only was it hard to live in Ethiopia, and the ministry was difficult, but her kids were also gone from home. Eventually, Mom thought she needed to speak with someone to get help. Dad was gone, and she felt she could not completely explain her feelings to him. She met with a missionary doctor and explained her situation. He felt she was a little depressed and gave her some meds to take to help. Then she began to feel that she was overweight and developed a poor self-image and shared that with the same physician. After some time and numerous visits, she was addicted to amphetamines that were given to help her temporarily. Sadly, she became addicted and could not seem to get off them.

She began to have some emotional and physical issues because of the meds she was taking. Dad would spend time asking her what was wrong, but she never revealed the problems or truth. She had withdrawals, but these were usually when Dad was gone. Even on furlough back in America, she could get the pills to which she was addicted. I remember as a second grader seeing her in bed for a few days at a time, but I did not know why. Later, I found out it was because she was having withdrawals. This went on for several years. Dad took her to see doctors, and they did tests wondering if this was some tropical disease or other sickness. She even went through brain scans, just going along with the whole thing and not telling Dad what was truly happening.

They somehow made it through furlough without the truth being revealed. Dad knew something was wrong, but he couldn't figure it out. Mom knew what was wrong but was afraid to tell him the truth. It was tough. Not only was she living in a remote place, usually by herself trying to do ministry with people who have never heard of Jesus, dealing with a low self-image, her kids away at boarding school, she was now addicted to medications that were supposed to help her get through all of it.

Years later, a friend asked her, "How did you make it through going to Ethiopia living in a tent, learning to cook in the ground, sending your kids to boarding school, dealing with health concerns while your husband was gone most of the time?" She responded, "It was hard, and unfortunately, I turned to drugs." But that is not the end of her story.

During their next term in Ethiopia after returning from furlough, Dad spent a lot of time praying and asking God for help and for answers. He knew they could not continue to go on with the way things were. In fact, he was thinking that they were probably returning to close out their ministry in Ethiopia. He had seen many other missionaries leave for many reasons, and most of them were family issues because Ethiopia was a difficult field.

Dad spoke with some of the Ethiopian leaders with whom he worked and asked them to pray for him and Mom. At the same time, Mom began dealing with the fact that she needed to tell the truth and get out of this addiction. Not only were her kids away from her, but now she had this stronghold. She needed to get over this so she could be there for her kids and be the mother she needed to be when they were home and when she and Dad visited the kids in school.

Dad had a Friday midweek prayer service since he was gone during the rest of the week helping with building projects. Usually, he would leave on Monday and return on Thursday if he could get away from the project. Then he would have his midweek prayer service on Friday, train leaders on Saturday, and have services on Sunday. So on the Friday midweek services, the people spent a lot of time in prayer. Dad began to mention Mom and her health to them, and they prayed fervently for her. Sometimes Mom was there at the prayer service, and other times she was not.

On one particular Friday, Dad went to the midweek prayer service while Mom stayed home. Dad shared his heart with them and asked them to keep praying because if things did not change, soon they would have to leave Ethiopia and return to America for good. The church people really concentrated on praying for her that night. When they prayed, they really prayed in faith and believed God was listening, and they literally wept and asked God to intervene. That service lasted a little longer than normal.

At the same time that they were praying, Mom was home praying, and she asked God to give her the courage and strength to tell the truth to my dad. She didn't want to hurt his ministry and testimony by revealing what was happening. However, she was now determined to tell him the truth when he returned home from the prayer meeting. She began to watch out the window for the car lights to show up. He was coming home later than usual, and she did not know why. It was because of the special time of prayer they had on her behalf. Finally, she saw the lights. Her heart began to beat rapidly, and her head began to hurt. Could she do this? She was getting very nervous. As the car approached the house, she opened the door and ran out to meet Dad with tears in her eyes. She said, "Richard, I have some important things to share with you. I don't know why, but my heart is telling me I must tell you now. I can't wait and put this off any longer."

They spoke to each other for hours through the night. They hugged each other, cried with each other, and began to discuss how to work through this addiction. Mom expressed that she wanted to work together and to stay in Ethiopia because God had called them there. They agreed to do this. They also agreed to spend more time with the kids for their sake and Mom's sake. It took two years to get off the amphetamines. There were some very difficult times during the process, but they committed to each other to do this for the sake of the Lord and for the sake of reaching the Ethiopians with the Gospel.

Mom later shared that although she read the Bible every day and prayed, she finally had to come to the point she could thank the Lord that her kids could go to boarding school and get a good education. The verses of Philippians 4:4–7 became very important to her:

> Rejoice in the Lord always: and again I say, Rejoice. Let your moderation be known unto all men. The Lord is at hand. Be careful for nothing; but in everything by prayer and supplication with thanksgiving let your requests be made known unto God. And the peace of God, which passeth all understanding, shall keep your hearts and minds through Christ Jesus.

She understood that she needed to rejoice in the Lord always, even when her kids were at school. Philippians also says to give thanks for everything, and that is what really helped her—giving thanks to God that her children could go to school, be with other missionary kids, and get a good education. And then verse 7 was key: "And the peace of God, which passeth all understanding, shall keep your hearts and minds through Christ Jesus."

She knew it was going to have to be God working in her and enabling her to make it. It was the peace of God that was going to help her keep her heart and mind in the right place before God, which can only be through Jesus Christ. Then she went on down to verse 13: "I can do all things through Christ which strengtheneth me."

This verse gave her the confidence knowing that Christ would be there with her and give her the strength to make it through the boarding school issue, the difficult living, hard ministry, and loneliness. Sure enough, all the glory goes to God for helping Mom and Dad make it through, serving God for many years to come as missionaries and seeing many Ethiopians come to know Christ as their Savior.

Kristina was born in 1970. That made eighteen years and three boys between the two girls. Mom was happy with the birth of Tina because it meant another child at home while the others were gone to school. When Eric went off to school, I was about one-year-old. When I went to school, there was no one. It was as if Mom wanted another child when the last one was ready to go to school or had already gone. Along came Kristina, or Tina, as we call her.

My parents said in their later years that if they could do it all over again, they would do more together as a family, especially when we were all home. Dad regrets building so much and even being gone when we were home from school. Don't take this wrong. It is not that they neglected us altogether. They did take us fishing at a swamp area where we could catch catfish. We also did picnics on occasion, and we went to some hot springs and swam and had a great time together.

Dad says it is important to give attention to your children on the mission field and to balance that with work. However, it doesn't always work to take two weeks off for every two weeks you work. Mission work is demanding and especially in those pioneer days. Plan your times together and set that time aside. Sometimes, we went to Bishaftu (Bih-shof-too), Lake Langano (Lawn-gone-oh), and Sodu for family times. The SIM made their missionaries take one month a year at Bishaftu for rest and relaxation. We could use that place too but never did for a whole month. It was a retreat area next to a volcanic lake. They had boats to row, the lake to swim in, and a peaceful, quiet retreat. My parents felt blessed because for the most part, we accepted boarding school and did okay. Some needed more care than others. You see, it all depends on the child and their personality needs, as well as school options.

In those days, missionaries were told to do God's work, and He will take care of your family. Therefore, many people put their ministry before their family. My dad was very consumed with the work, and he admits he did neglect his family. Dad advises people to give time to family and kids and extra time as necessary. Keep them ahead of the ministry and let them know they are important. There were so many different pressures and difficulties in Ethiopia. Many families struggled.

CHAPTER SEVEN

Our Mountain

After a lot of prayer and seeking God's direction for the mission station that my parents would start, they determined it was going to be near Kombolcha (Come-bowl-chuh). Kombolcha is town about four hours farther north from Robi. It has several mountain ranges around the town and is a little higher in altitude, so it is not quite as hot as Robi. About an hour farther north is a larger town called Dessi. Dessi has stores and two hospitals. That is the town where a limited amount of supplies for living and building could be obtained. There were missionaries with other groups who operated a hospital and leprosarium. Dessie was near the top of one of the mountain ranges, and the roads were very winding going up the mountainside. There were parts of the road that were scary as you would be looking down thousands of feet, and the road was not always very wide. Kombolcha is in the valley below and has a river called Borkena (Bore-ken-ah) going through it. There was an airstrip where DC 3 airplanes would occasionally land and bring supplies along with a few passengers. We all loved the area. It was a beautiful mountainous location.

This was in a predominantly Muslim area. Our mission station was situated outside of Kombolcha about three kilometers south in a village of mud huts called Abish Agur, which means "grain country." Mr. Cain found about a half an acre of land. My dad went with Mr. Cain to work on getting this property. They, through much negotiating back and forth, finally got the owner, Mohammed, to lease us that land for thirty years. We eventually increased the size we leased to one acre.

Mr. Cain had a tent he pitched, and he usually took one or two Ethiopians around with him. He lived very frugally when he went to these places. To complete the agreement, he also had to obtain permission from the local government. Once that was obtained, we put up a barbed-wire fence around the one-acre piece of land and started to build our three-roomed pioneer unit. Our mission station was divided into three sections and had a slight slope down toward the river where each section was lower than the other. On the upper side, closest to the village, was the school. This is where the schoolchildren played and where ladies eventually came to get their water.

There was a hedgerow to separate the school area from our house and the home of another missionary. The houses were on the second section. We planted nice thick grass that covered this entire area. Dad planted a pine tree in the middle of the two houses that grew very tall. At night, we lay on the grass and watched the stars. On some nights, we could see the satellites go by in orbit. It was so clear and dark. In 1969, the news spread all the way to the countryside of Ethiopia that America had sent a man who landed on the moon. The local Muslims didn't believe it because their Imams told them that was impossible. They were told that their god, Allah, had promised the moon to the Muslims, and someday they would all live up there. Therefore, they never believed the news of the moon landing.

One time, we got three baby warthogs from Robi. We thought we could raise them as pets. They mainly lived under this pine tree in the center of our yard. They felt very secure there. For some unknown reason, they got sick with diarrhea, so Mom tried to help them and gave them kaopectate. It killed them all.

On the third section of the mission station below the missionary houses, we kept our mules and horse for visitation into the mountain villages. We also had a chicken coop there. Eventually, we had a barn built for the animals.

My parents began to prepare the land and get it ready to become a mission station for a home, school, and church. Dad was trying to find rocks and stones to put in the driveway that went from the main road down through a small part of the village to the entrance of our mission station. After a short time, the village people began complaining that Dad was taking the rocks out of their farmland. These rocks would help during the rains and make a good driveway for us. He also thought that it would help their farmland by getting rid of the rocks. They complained and said that the rocks were for fertilizer and helped keep their soil in place, so he had to get the rocks from somewhere else. Soon Dad started to build our pioneer unit. They still lived in the tent while building it. Mom continued cooking on her one-burner camping stove, and here she even learned to make pies in a hole in the ground. She was amazing.

This was where my parents started their spiritual work along with a school. Dad went out from here to other new mission stations north and south to help build houses and schools. Our pioneer unit was just like the others with three rooms. However, at first, my dad built the kitchen and storage section and the bedroom section. Both rooms were on each end, so before the middle room was finished, they placed planks from one to the other that spanned ten feet between and two feet off the ground. That is what they walked on to get from one room to the other. When it was finished, most of us slept in the same room except for Ole. He slept with Dad on the couch in the remaining room. The tin on the walls went up halfway and then screen the rest of the way up.

Our pioneer unit was on stilts about twenty-four inches off the ground so we could crawl underneath to check for termites. Ole liked to dig tunnels under the pioneer unit. Once, Dad was having a hole dug for the outhouse nearby. It had only been dug to four feet deep. Ole told Eric to get in the hole. He then put boards over the top of the hole and then put dirt on top of the boards. At suppertime, Eric wasn't there. When Mom found out where Eric was and what

Ole had done, she was mad. She said, "What if a horse walked over that and fell in and landed on Eric?" Needless to say, Ole was in big trouble.

The villagers near the station lived mainly in mud huts with grass thatched roofs and walls made of cornstalks connected to a few main poles made of eucalyptus trees. Eucalyptus trees were said to have been brought over from Australia. They grew quickly. They could cut them down once they got to the size of a telephone pole, and in seven years, they were back to that original size. They tied these together with pieces of sisal. Then they plastered over those cornstalks with a mixture of mud and cow manure. They mixed this with chaff or grain in a big pit and put water in it. They would walk about in it with bare feet for about four days to mix it. It made good plaster and could be smoothed out quite nicely. After it dried, it did not smell. Inside the huts, there was an internal wall for their cows, sheep, and goats to stay in at night. Their animals were kept in that space between the outer wall and the inner wall, which was about four feet wide. The people lived in the smaller area in the center. They would have a fire where they did their cooking. It was an open fire in the middle of the hut. They slept on the ground or on a bed-frame of wood with metal straps and a blanket to lay on or a sack stuffed with grass. The roofs were made of grass, and the smoke from the fire went out through a hole at the top of the center pole. The pole went up through the roof's cap-like vent. Most had a bench on the side wall to sit on and/or sleep on at night. I went into their huts all the time. It was usually quite dark and sometimes very smoky. It was fun to eat their local food in their homes. It is called *injera* and *watt*. It is characteristically eaten without using utensils and consists of vegetable and meat sauces (watt) with sourdough bread (injera). The spongy bread is used to scoop up the sauces. Some of the sauces are spicy with chicken, beef, lamb, and lintels. The food is very tasty and savory. Some of it was so spicy hot that I would sweat, and my nose would run. It was so good! *Injera* and *watt* is my favorite food.

The climate was warm but comfortable at 6,400 feet elevation. It was not humid. The winter and summer seasons were opposite from America. The big rains came usually from April through June, and the light rains later in the fall. The mountains and the valleys were all cultivated for corn, grain, and some vegetables. The people knew when to plow and plant throughout the year.

Once, the rains started coming for two weeks and then quit, which was very unusual. So Dad prepared our garden to take advantage of those rains. He asked the farmers why they weren't planting. "You might get an extra crop," he said. They disagreed and said, "That is not the way we do it." A few weeks later, Dad saw that the grass on the mountainside was starting to turn brown. Everything was dying, and the coloring was moving toward the village. It was a caterpillar worm eating everything. This happened when the rains started early, and the caterpillars ate everything in sight. The condition came all the way to our station and village. Dad put insecticide on our garden, and the bugs went around it. As the worms reached the river, they died off. Immediately after that, the people started planting their crops. They knew how all this worked.

In our garden, we grew strawberries, carrots, beets, lettuce, and beans. The water we eventually brought in the pipes down the mountain helped to keep it going. We had banana, papaya, and guava trees around our station.

We had a dog named Fluffy. Dad was not happy when we got the dog because he knew the Muslims did not like dogs. He did not want to hinder our potential to reach them with the Gospel. We were told it was an Italian shepherd. We got her because I was afraid of dogs. If any man, woman, or child came out of school and crossed the hedgerow, the dog would bite them. My dad had to medically dress quite a few dog-bite wounds. Whenever Fluffy would run into the school yard, all the kids would sit down. If they sat down, the dog didn't bite them; she just slowly walked around them and looked for food. Sometimes the kids gave her a little food. Fluffy could go to the village and walk around by their huts and would never bother the villagers. The people were okay with this. The only thing that would make her mad was the shepherds that teased her when walking toward the river on the path next to our station. Sometimes she even chased hyenas at night. The villagers thought she was part human.

Not long after our pioneer unit was built, I was born. No, I wasn't born in this house, but my parents had gone to the capital city, Addis Ababa, for my birth. I was born in a small hospital located on some land right behind the emperor's palace. It was called the Empress Zewditu (Zo-dee-too) Hospital. Mom never expressed her fear of me being born in Ethiopia. She always placed her trust in the Lord. She sometimes traveled to Addis with Darlene Clark to see the doctor during her pregnancy with me. Other times, she could see the American doctor at the Seventh Day Adventist Hospital in Dessi. Darlene had become a close friend with Mom. They really enjoyed each other's company.

My parents made some good inroads into the village. At first, the villagers were not sure about these foreigners and the mission station they built. They weren't antagonistic but mainly curious. When I was about three weeks old and was then home in Kombolcha, the ladies wanted to see this newborn baby—especially a white one. My mom walked into the village, and thirty ladies lined up to come by and see me. Mom held me out in her arms, and they each came by, one by one, to see this new baby. They each did something Mom was not expecting. They each came by and spat on me! When the first one did it, Mom was startled and shocked! She wanted to turn and run. She was concerned for her newborn and what I might be exposed to. However, she thought that if she was to ever reach those ladies with the Gospel, she could not run. So she stayed there holding me out for all thirty of them to come by and spit on me. Later, she found out they did this culturally for two reasons: The first reason was their special way to give their blessings upon a newborn. The second reason was to keep evil spirits away from this baby. They lived in great fear of the devil and his spirits, and so they did all kinds of things to keep them away.

At the end of our second four-year term, my dad finished our cement blockhouse. It took a while because he would leave this project to help others build their homes. The BBFI gave $5,000 to put together a mission station. To open our station and build the pioneer unit cost $1,000. Then Dad built the first classroom with cement blocks for the church/school that cost $1,000. When the time came to build our main house, we only had $3,000 left to build it. Near the bridge going into town, there was a man who made cement blocks, and we bought some there. They were not bad, but he did not use enough cement, so they were kind of fragile and broke easily. Dad had to plaster them on both the inside and outside to help make them stronger. The house was twenty-five feet by thirty-five feet. The windows had metal frames with clear glass panes. My dad taught a few of his hired helpers how to mix cement with sand and place it in a single block maker he acquired. After mixing the cement, they would put the mix into the mold and then let it dry. They took the block out and stacked it with others and then put in more mix. My dad finished our new house and made many other buildings for schools and churches by making one block at a time. This house had a tin room. I remember the noise in the daytime from the pigeons walking on the peak of the roof and how annoying it was—even with a ceiling inside. Dad said we could shoot the pigeons with our pellet and BB guns as long as we did not shoot the doves. The house had a nice kitchen for Mom with a gas stove and kerosene refrigerator. The kitchen cabinets and sink formed a *U* shape—near the back door. The cabinets on the wall across from the open part of the U went from floor to the ceiling for storage and a pantry.

For a while, when Mom cooked in the kitchen or would wash the dishes, there was a little yellow bird that would come peck at her on the window. This happened for quite a while, and then a few months later, it never came around again. We figured it must have been one of the birds I shot during one of my many "hunting expeditions." Mom was not happy about that.

There were two bedrooms, plus one more room for the bathroom. There was a living room and dining area. The floors were made of tongue and groove cedar wood from Addis. This was good because the termites would not eat the cedar wood. In the living room, we had a nice fireplace that Dad built using his experience as a bricklayer in Denver. The brick went from one side to the other side of the living room. There was a marble hearth ten inches above the floor that came out about sixteen inches. It was a great place to sit on. We only used the fireplace at Christmas because it was normally too warm. My parents stayed in one bedroom, and all four kids stayed in the other bedroom. At first, we were all in the one room. The boys slept in the same bed, and Jacque slept in one by herself. One time, Ole woke up with his side wet. He wondered how in the world that happened. He thought he had wet the bed, but he hadn't done that in years. Then he noticed he was only wet on his side. I had wet the bed.

Finally, my dad built triple bunks for the boys. My bed was on the bottom, Eric's in the middle, and Ole's on top. Ole's was close to the ceiling, and he could hear the lizards and rats scurrying up above in the ceiling. He eventually could tell which one was which. My dad built a two-sided bookshelf for the middle of the room, and Jacque slept on the other side of that in her own bed. Eventually, Jacque moved to the small room in the middle that was supposed to be an inside bathroom. That room was never totally completed.

On the west end of the house, there was a small door built to get into the crawlspace under the house. This crawlspace was used for two reasons: first was to be able to check for any termites around the foundation and floor; the second reason was for storage. Also, at that end of the house was a grease pit with a concrete driveway to drive up on. This is where Dad could stand and work on the bottom of a car. A wooden board was placed over the opening to the pit when not being used. Once this house was completed, our pioneer unit became our guesthouse and storage.

We always used an outhouse as a restroom. It was usually located about ten to fifteen yards away from the house. The outhouses were usually built to sit on two beams so they could be carried and moved to a newly dug hole. One of the first ones we had was suspended over a large hole. The problem was the side walls of the hole were caving in slowly. When Dr. Donnelson visited, he needed to use it. He said it was scary walking out there to that "island." Another time, we had a rooster that always liked to somehow get into the outhouse. Once, Mr. Cain was traveling north; and when he got to our station, he stopped to go to the restroom. He walked to our outhouse and saw this rooster sitting in there. It made a mean noise at him. He turned around and got in his car and continued his trip north to the next station. That rooster was known for being mean and always chased us kids around. I was never sure how it got into the outhouse.

The last outhouse we had was fairly nice. It was a two-seater. That was like being modern with luxury. One seat was taller for the adults, and next to it was a seat lower for the kids. It was painted green on the inside. The outside walls were made of tin. Of course, it was always an ordeal when we had to dig a new hole and move the outhouse to a new location.

It was kind of scary at night going to the bathroom because it was usually near our barbed-wire fence. Right outside the fence, you could hear hyenas making their noises at night. As a kid, that was very scary. So we called for the night guard, and he would come and stand near us as we would "go number one" off the porch. It was always bad if you had to "go number two," and he would have to walk with you to the outhouse shining his flashlight. We thought he was good protection.

Mom was leaving for what would be our last furlough, departing a short time before my dad left. She went with the other kids, and I remained with my dad to return for furlough with him later. On the way to the airport, Mom said to Dad, "You build houses for the other missionaries and always put in a bathroom for them. Do you think you could do that for us?" She wasn't complaining but only inquiring. My dad said, "I'm going to do that before I leave for furlough." On the way back from the airport, he bought all the plumbing to do the job. He began to fix up the bathroom, putting in a commode, a tub, and the necessary plumbing. He dug a cesspool out in the back. He got close to getting it all together, but there was one part he forgot to get—an elbow with a drain plug for the toilet. So he had all that done when we left to go home on furlough. When the communists took over the country, our family didn't return, and we never lived in that house again.

Near our house, Dad built a flat tin building that had his workshop on one end. The next room housed a diesel generator. After that was a small room for his office where he would study the language and prepare Bible lessons. Then there was a small area for a shower and a room to do laundry by hand.

The generator was so helpful for using some power tools and lights at night. I remember how cool it was when Dad made an "on and off" switch in his bedroom. When it started to get dark, we could push the green button to turn on the generator, and then around 9:00 p.m., he pushed the red button to turn it off.

One of our night guards was named Yimir (Yee-mir). He was our guard for a long time. He carried a .22 rifle, and I think he had one or two bullets. I always asked to see his bullet, and he reluctantly pulled it out of his pocket and showed me. He often slept at night, and it was hard to find him. He always wore a green heavy coat that seemed to me to be way too hot.

Yimir worked for us for a long time. My dad sometimes went out at night to see Yimir, and he would be lying in the grass, sleeping.

So to have fun and perhaps teach him that he needed to be careful, Dad took his flashlight and walked back into the house. In the morning, he would come to turn in his flashlight and .22 rifle. He'd say, "I don't know what happened to the flashlight." My dad would say, "Did it look like this?" He realized Dad caught him sleeping. This happened a good amount of time. Yimir never got mad, but I don't know if he ever learned what my dad was trying to teach him. If he fell asleep, thieves would do worse things to him.

Our village did not have running water. That means our mission station didn't have it either. Dad tried to dig and build a well. They went thirty-five feet deep and six feet in diameter, but they never hit water. When digging the well, the workers went down into it by rope, dug a little, and put the dirt in a bucket and sent it up one bucket at a time. Sometimes the sides would start to cave in. So Dad took one by six inch boards and built braces to hold the walls up. It was also dark down there because it was so deep. People would come by and yell at the workers, saying, "You are going to die!" We yelled back, "No, you won't." We were praying every day that God would protect them. The men made forty cents a day to dig this well, which was five cents over the norm. Unfortunately, they never hit water and so it had to be filled in again. Before they filled it in, Dad said they needed to take the wood out. They refused because they were afraid it would cave in. Dad went down himself, loosened up all the boards, and sent them up by rope, and was fine.

We had to get our water from a small spring that came from the mountain. It was a quarter of a mile away from our station. It was the community water place where everyone got their water. In addition to that, the cows would get in it, and the people washed clothes in it. That was the only option we had. We would go get a few buckets of water, carry it home, and then boil it for twenty minutes. My parents often said, "If we don't have diarrhea at least once a week, we must be sick."

My dad came up with a great idea. Across the main road, there was a small mountain range. He went up the mountain quite a way and found where a spring was coming out of the ground. Dad got permission from the local government to encase that spring in a cement casement. He brought three-quarter-inch piping all the way down to our station. It was not an easy task and took some interesting ingenuity.

They built the encasement to hold the water. They dug a trench from there all the way down the mountainside for the pipes to lay in. It was probably several thousand feet down to the main road. They had to pass through three different property owners' land. When they got to one man's land, he stopped them and said, "You can't come across my land. In the name of Haile Selassie, you can't cross my land!" But we had permission from the government to bring the pipe down. He didn't budge, so they went on the other side of that man's land and started digging a trench across other people's land who did not object.

Eventually, they came to the main road. They had to cross it. The big Fiat trucks driven by Italians kept coming, so they had to dig halfway across the road, put the pipe down, and fill that ditch back in. Then they dug the other half until they crossed the road. Before they got the pipe to the mission station, another man began to object to the project. He went to the police, and he brought the head policeman. When the policeman saw what was being done, he said, "You cannot dig across this man's land. You can't do that." He gave us a hard time for a while as Dad tried to tell him we had permission. But the policeman wouldn't listen. He wanted a bribe, but Dad wouldn't give in to him. This stalled the project once again.

One night, we heard the shouting and yelling of many voices. This was the way the villagers would sound an alarm of help and emergency. When we ran outside our pioneer unit, we could see huge flames in a field next to the village. We ran toward the flames with a couple of men from the village and saw a huge stack of teff on fire. Teff is a grain the villagers used to make their bread. The burning teff belonged to the man who brought the police to complain about the water project. We went up with our buckets and started helping.

Men formed a line from the stream and passed buckets of water. Every time my dad got a bucket, he handed it directly to the owner. The man could not believe Dad would help after what he had done to stop the water project. Eventually, they got the fire out and saved most of his grain. The next day, he came down when we were working on the pipe and said, "It's okay now. You can go across my land." My dad believed God was in that situation because it was not looking very promising. How had the fire started? No one knew, and they never did find out.

We finally had water into our home, for the entire station, and for the school. Then my dad made a place on the station where the women could carry their heavy clay pots and fill them with water. He built a platform to set their pots on. After it was filled, they could put them on their backs without having to lift them as much. The filled pots probably weighed fifty pounds. They were happy because they no longer had to bend over and lift the pots or help each other to lift them. They carried the water back to their mud homes in the village. Oftentimes, kids would bring different-sized cans to carry water back home. Sometimes the line would be long waiting to get water, and there was a lot of visiting going on among the ladies. I used to enjoy going around there and playing with the kids as they waited with their mothers. This was a great way to assist the community and show the love of God. It made for a great way to visit with, and witness to, the people.

After we lived in this village and close to the town of Kombolcha for a while, the people got used to us and began to trust us. They saw the things we did to help the community with water, the school, and other ways. My dad also did a lot of first aid, but it ended up being more. Dad knew first aid from being on the fire department for five years in Denver. Most of the people came because of what we called tropical ulcers. These are skin lesions or infections thought to be caused by microorganisms. It is a very common condition in tropical climates. People would accidentally cut themselves, or maybe get cut on a bush, and flies would land on those wounds, infecting them. A nurse at the SIM leprosarium near Dessi, about an hour away, told my dad the best way to clean out these ulcers. She told him to treat any infected area with a mix of Epsom salts and salve or Vaseline. She said to smear that mixture on the sores and put a bandage on it. Then have them come back in a day or two, sprinkle sulphur powder on the wound, put a bandage on it again, and have them come back in a couple of days. Repeat the process a third time, and it would heal shortly. It usually worked.

The kids had flies on their eyes most of the time, even on their nose or in their nose. These flies caused conjunctivitis for many people. It would make them unable to see, so my dad used eye ointment for that purpose. He opened their eyelids and applied ointment in their eyes. He would have them come back every day. In a short time, it would be gone. What happened to many is that their eyelid began to fold under. The eyelashes began to scrape up and down on the eyeball. It can cause blindness. If they didn't have this treatment or go to the hospital in Dessi, they would end up going blind.

The local Muslim Imam came to speak with Dad because my dad helped people with these wounds. He was surprised at the care Dad provided for all the people, even the Muslims. He didn't understand his own religion very much as my dad asked him questions and tried to witness to him. One day, the Imam's wife came to see Dad because she had contracted conjunctivitis. She had been to one of the witch doctors for help. He took a razor blade and tried to cut the eyelash root off her eyelid. The result was when she closed her eyes, there was a small slit that let in the light and unfortunately dirt too. She was having a lot of problems with that. It got to an extreme point where my dad could not help her.

The people used an open fire in the center of the hut for cooking and heat. During the night, an older man rolled over into the fire while he was sleeping. He had waited awhile before coming to see Dad. When he did come, he had a huge scab on his whole back. My dad got his famous Epsom salt, and he pulled the scab back away from the body and doused it down inside the scab. He was afraid to pull it all off and didn't want to expose all the skin. Also, there were maggots crawling around underneath the scab. In the old days, they used maggots to clean out dead flesh, so my dad decided to leave the maggots. After a week or so, the scab came off, and he could then use this Epsom salt and salve to continue the healing. It worked.

One man had several camels that he used to bring up slabs of salt from the Red Sea and the Indian Ocean. Sometimes his camels got sick or got wounds. A couple of times, he brought these camels for Dad to doctor. He put medicine on them, and the man thought it was just wonderful. Dad doctored all kinds of things.

There was a man brought in on a stretcher from across the river. He had a bad sore on his right side. The missionary nurse from the leprosarium was visiting, and she looked at it. She told him he had tuberculosis. She told him that if he would come to leprosarium, they could treat him and help him. They talked about how much money it would cost to get there. Someone asked if he had a cow or something to sell to get the bus fare. He said he had one cow. His friends said, "He's very sick, and we can't sell his cow because if he dies, we need the cow to feed people who come to his funeral." The man never went. We are not sure what happened to him.

An older man came all the way from Dessi. There was a government hospital and a Seventh Day Adventist hospital in that town. He passed those hospitals and rode the bus for an hour to come to our area. My dad asked him why he didn't just go to one of those hospitals. He replied, "It is your hand that heals, not the medicines." This was the perfect opportunity to share with him about the Great Physician.

One family brought their little girl to see Dad. She was trying to milk a donkey. The animal did not like that and kicked her in the forehead. It cut her forehead and made a hoof impression in her skull. My dad tried to convince them to take her to the hospital. They refused and only came back to see him until the cut was cured. You could still see the scar and the hoof indention in her skull. She grew up and eventually got married. She had a few kids of her own.

Some men came with wounds from axes as they cut down trees. Dad became very popular, and every morning, people would line up outside his tool shop to be treated for all these various wounds. I would sit and watch as he doctored them and sent them on their way. They usually came back for more treatments. This was another way my dad showed the love of God by helping people free of charge so that he would gain the opportunity to share the Gospel with them.

We did not have a telephone, so to make a call to the United States, we went to town to this little yellow building that held about three people—the operator and two guests. We would go make our request to call a number in Addis Ababa. Then the operator would tell us to come back in a couple of hours, or sometimes we would sit there and wait. The operator had a crank-type telephone. He cranked it until he reached the operator in the next town. The operator there called the next town and exchange, who connected to the next town and exchange, until they connected with the capital city. It was a long ordeal, and by the time we got to speak, it was only for a very short time. It cost a lot to make the call, and most of the time, it got cut off. We did not do this very often. It was too much of a hassle.

Many Italian truck drivers, mechanics, and contractors remained in Ethiopia after the war with Italy. The emperor asked them to help Ethiopia become more modern. In Kombolcha, there were three Italian families we befriended. One family owned the Agip gas station, which also had a restaurant with good spaghetti, lasagna, and other homemade Italian food. They were very nice people and quite helpful in so many ways. They didn't speak English or Amharic, and we didn't know Italian. But somehow, through hand motions and a few words here and there, we were able to communicate. Some of their kids became our friends, and it was fun to visit them. The other two families had a garage to repair cars and machines. Senior

Rosmo owned and managed the garage. We knew his boys Etory, Hector, and Ellio. Ellio was my age, and the other two were older. They learned to be good mechanics too. It was fun to hang around their garage.

The government required that our missionaries have schools to teach the children how to read and write, along with math and other subjects. We had to do this to be able to have the mission stations. These took a lot of time at first, until teachers and administrators could be trained and equipped to take the schools forward. Eventually, we had a pretty good-sized school up through the sixth grade.

The local families sent their children to our school, knowing we would provide a good education. Some of the kids in the first grade were eighteen years old because they had never been to school. The rules required them to arrive at school on time. There was the morning gathering at the flagpole. Each class had to get in their line and stand straight and tall. The teachers walked up and down the lines to take roll and make sure the students were dressed properly. Then the teachers stood at the front as they all sang their national anthem. I often went to watch this and stand at the front with the teachers. It wasn't that I was anybody special. It was what I was going to witness. If any student was late, they could not get in line but had to come to the front before all the other students. Then the latecomer had to bend over and grab his or her ankles. The school leader had a board in his hands, and he spanked the student hard with the board for being late. I don't remember any of them crying out loud, but I could tell it hurt. By the way, the parents were all for it and were even glad for it. They said it assured them that they knew their children would learn to be to school on time and not play around. The parents backed up this effort one hundred percent. Sometimes when the kids misbehaved at home, we'd have parents bring them and ask us to paddle them. They wanted their children to behave. Of course, we did not do that for them.

In the first classroom Dad built and where the school started, Eric and I would host a "film night." We had old 16mm films of Abbott and Costello, Geronimo, and others to show. We went around the village that afternoon and yelled out that we were going to show a film. Most of the people had never seen anything like this before, and of course, they did not understand what they were watching. Eric charged people to enter the room to watch the films. He thought he could make some money doing this. The place would end up being full of kids, and Eric always ended up with very little money. I was to be the one to collect the money. I guess I didn't do a good job, and the kids would just force their way in. They loved to watch them, although most of them did not understand what they were about.

After being at this mission station for a few months, my dad began to hire people to help with keeping up the mission station and with building projects. We had a night guard, a lady who helped around the house, and three men to help with the grounds and building projects. Some of them had to be taught the basics.

What I liked is that these helpers became like family. We would be with them often. They brought their lunch in small metal containers. They ate the local bread (injera) mixed with different sauces (watt). Boy, did it taste good. I would sit with them outside and eat their lunches with them. They were always so generous and gracious. I got to learn the language better this way, and the food was an added benefit.

One of our first helpers was a man named Emom (Ee-mom). He suddenly decided he didn't want to work with us. We were never sure what happened to him. Some believed he left because of problems with his wife. We never saw him again. There were two other faithful ones who helped us. One was Ababa (Ah-buh-buh). He worked a lot around the station cutting grass, digging ditches, repairing fences, and he learned to make the cement blocks for building. The other one was Amaday (Ahh-muh-day), who knew a little bit about building. He was a good man and was more experienced and learned to do things quickly. Like most others, he came from a Muslim background. Soon after working with us, he trusted Christ and followed God in every way. He was an honest man and helped my dad in so many ways. He went with dad to work on the other mission stations as well.

Ababa was older, and he had to cross the river to come to work. Once, he was crossing the river during the rainy season, and the river was violent. He was carrying his young child on his shoulder. The water hit him and knocked him over, and he lost his little girl. She drowned and went down the river. I don't know if they ever found her body.

Ababa and Amaday were precious people to us. Ababa liked to joke and play around with my siblings and me, especially Ole. One time, my dad needed a tool and told him to get it from the tool shed. He didn't know where it was, so he went to Ole for help. Ole was not even a teenager yet. Ababa said, "Your dad wants this tool. Do you know where this tool is? If I don't take him this tool, he'll kick me in the bottom." I don't know if Ole found it for him or not. My dad never kicked him, and we have laughed about that many times.

These men were very helpful to Mom. When she needed things from the market, they got them for her. The market was an open-air market that was held on Wednesdays and Saturdays a few miles away. There was also a butcher shop. It was a one-room butcher shop. You knew there was new meat when they hung the esophagus and lungs of a cow on the door. That was their notice that they had fresh meat available. It was usually tough, though. Normally it was killed, purchased, and eaten on the same day since we did not have refrigeration at first.

We had various night guards. Some of them would last a little longer than others. When my dad was going back and forth into Robi, he would be gone for five or six days. One night, while he was gone, someone came to the pioneer unit and tried to open the door. Mom asked, "Who's there?" They ran off. She opened the door and went out to call the night guard. We had a little three by three foot guard shack that the guards sat in when it was raining. Well, this guy was sitting in there and had fallen asleep. When Mom hollered, he came running and got excited after Mom told him someone came and knocked on the door. He ran all around the station, scared of who was out there and who had come to open the door. He was more scared than my mom was.

There were thieves around, but they did not usually bother us. One night, someone broke into the house and stole our only radio out of the front room. When my dad heard the noise, he got up and started chasing the guy in the night all the way down to the river. He never did catch or find him. That was the only problem we had with thieves in the night.

Hyenas are scavengers. They look for easy prey. We would come home from church on Sunday or Friday night and park the car near our house. Dad sometimes got out his strong spotlight and shone it over onto the huts on the edge of the village. We could see hyenas walking around the huts trying to see if they could grab a goat or cow or even a child. They were scary. We lay in our beds at night and listened to the hyenas make their unique, peculiar noise. It was always strange to me that they came out at night and stayed in their holes in the ground during the day.

The people were afraid of the hyenas. Some believed that the devil rode around on them at night, causing problems for people and the village. They believed the hyena was the *horse of the devil.*

One night, Dad decided to go out and shoot a hyena. They were bothering the villagers and their animals. Dad was not really a hunter like some of the other missionaries. He took his .22 rifle. He knew it didn't always work well, and sometimes it even misfired. Dad made his way out of our station to where he saw some hyena eyes glowing in the distance. It was dark. He got closer to the eyes and lifted the gun to shoot. He stared down the sights and aimed between a set of eyes glancing his way. He steadied his aim and pulled the trigger. The gun misfired! Now the pack of them were looking his way because of the noise the gun made. Fortunately, for my dad, they decided to run away. He later got to thinking this probably wasn't very wise because there ended up being about ten of them out there. In a pack, they are dangerous. If he injured one, the rest might attack. He said he felt God protected him that night.

Gordon Wright, another BBFI missionary, would find roadkill along the main road and saw opportunities with that. He would pick it up and take it home. Usually, it was a goat that had been run over. He used it as bait for hunting hyenas. His method was to tie the dead animal at the base of a tree. He liked to take Eric and me with him. Boy, was that ever exciting! We helped tie it to the tree, and then as darkness came, we climbed up into the tree with him. Gordon pushed the play button on his tape player. It was a recording of laughing hyenas. The player was hooked up to a loud speaker. When the hyenas heard the laughing, they would come, thinking there must be food. As long as we stayed in the tree, we were safe. He would aim his gun down at them. I placed my fingers in my ears. *Boom*, the hyena would be shot. The next day, he would dig a hole and bury the animal. They were dirty scavenger animals, and you wouldn't keep the skins or anything.

The river that was below our mission station and ran near the town was called Borkena (Bor-ken-ah). Borkena is one of the tributaries of the Awash River draining eastward from the highlands of the Wollo (Wuh-low) province. The Borkena River flows for many miles from the mountains where we lived down to a swamp several hours down the road. Our mules and horses were taken to this river most days to graze. The area had a place that was like a community pasture. Many shepherd boys were there in the daytime with their sheep and cows.

It was a fun place to go play with the kids and their animals. At one place, the water ran under the grass. The grass was so intertwined and thick so that it would hold together, and you could walk on it while the river ran under it. We also did a lot of hunting there for different kinds of birds and other small animals. After hanging around those shepherd boys down by the river, Eric really wanted to become a shepherd.

We did some swimming in the river. There were places where big boulders made some swift rapids. Above those rapids were pools to swim in. Some parts were dangerous. Thankfully, we never got hurt. I believe it was God who was always watching over us—in answer to my mom's prayers.

Growing up on that mission station was an adventure. Since we had the school there, we had kids from all over the place. We played a lot with the local kids. We went all over the countryside with those who were not working as shepherds and when school was out. Everywhere we went, the kids knew our names and would yell them out. The town's kids were not as friendly as the village kids.

There were about eight to ten from the village who became my best friends. They had never seen toys like the ones I owned. I had some toy cars and other things that were intriguing to them. When Dad had a building project, he always had sandpiles around. Those made for good areas to play with the cars, so I would line up the ten boys and one or two girls. Then I pointed to the ones who could come and play that day. I did not have enough toys for everyone, so I had to choose. The others had to go do something else. It was always interesting with our dog, Fluffy. She was a smart dog. If one of the kids who had not been chosen tried to come and play, she would growl at them and act like she was going to bite them. The kids were afraid of our dog. They thought it was part human because it seemed so smart and would obey our commands.

When I was about seven years old, I noticed that some of my friends were eating something. It looked interesting to me, so I went over to see what it was. They were eating some dark dirt. They weren't eating a lot but just pieces. They asked me to try it. I did, and I remember thinking it was not too bad. I am not sure of the nutrient factor in it, but it did fill the stomach. One time, I had a little on my face when I went home, and Mom asked what I had been eating. When I told her, she gasped and couldn't believe it. She told me to stop. I said we had been doing it for a while, and they always did it—and it tasted good. She warned me again not to do it anymore. Although disappointed, I never did eat that dirt again.

My brothers had pellet and BB guns. When they went off to school, I got to hunt with those guns. Or they were just handed down to me when Ole and Eric were done with them. Usually, the barrels were bent, and the guns did not shoot straight. I went out with my friends to hunt for birds. I had to aim to the right of the bird a few inches since the barrel was bent to the left. I rarely hit a bird with the pellet gun. However, my friends threw rocks at the same time and oftentimes hit the birds. Sometimes I thought I shot the bird with the gun when it was actually hit with their rock.

When I had finally gotten the BB gun, I accidentally shot one of my friends in the leg. The gun held fifty BBs, but when you got down to the last two, you couldn't see them. Unless you were counting, it was hard to know if there were two or one left. I thought it was empty and aimed it at his leg. He yelled, "No." I said there was no BB in it. He kept yelling, so to show him it was empty, I pulled the trigger. Well, there was one left, and it really stung him in the upper leg.

We played games with the school kids during recess or PE. They had one game where they got in a circle, blindfolded two kids, and placed a belt on the ground somewhere inside the circle. The two blindfolded kids had to walk in the circle to find the belt. When one found it, they could go and swing the belt at the other one. They would whack them a few times until the other one could grab it and hold on. It was kind of a strange game. They played a game like dodgeball with a rubber ball or sock ball. They liked to play tag and chase each other too.

I had a good number of Ethiopian friends, and I went into their huts with them and ate in their homes. The names of some of them were Indirees, Said Ahamed, Amino Mekonnen, Iyalio, Fontu, and Ali Mekonnen. We played all day long together. Even when I went off to school and returned home for summer break, we would pick up right where we left off.

Across the river and valley from our mission station was a tall mountain. It had a nice shape to it, being wide at the base and forming toward a point at the top. When you looked closely, it appeared as one mountain. However, at the base of it was another mountain about halfway up. On the backside of the front mountain, it connected to the back mountain whose top went above the front mountain. Looking straight on at it, it looked like one mountain. It was taller than all the other mountains around the area. Some of the Ethiopians thought if you made it to the top, you could see the lights in America.

We called it *our mountain*. If you were not sure where you were, you could look for "*our mountain*" and know what direction to go. When we were on our twelve-hour drive home from boarding school, we always looked ahead for the mountain. When we saw it, we yelled, "There's our mountain!" and that meant we were almost home.

Some of the people believed that Satan lived on the mountain. They would go there and make burnt sacrifices to the devil. There were also stone walls near the top. They were old and grown over by grass. Some trenches were dug as well. When the country was divided into several territories, the different people groups set up these fortifications to fight one another and protect their territory.

Ole was the first one of us to go to the top of "*our mountain*" with Ababa. It was a full day's journey to go up and back. Eric also climbed it twice with some of his Ethiopian friends. I went up it a couple of times too. On one of my expeditions up the mountain, I saw an albino baboon. As soon as it saw me and my friends, it took off. We tried to follow it for a while but never saw it again.

In the early '70s, the government built a dirt road that went about three-quarters of the way to the top of the mountain. It went around the back side. My dad drove us up there once with my sister Tina, my friend Iyalio (Eye-yah-leo), and Ababa in our Land Rover. Once a year, the local people sacrificed a red heifer at the base of the mountain to worship Satan. Our idea for driving up there and staying the night in sleeping bags was so we could tell the people we stayed there and didn't see Satan. Dad told them we would find out and let them know. We stayed there overnight, and when we came back to the mission station, the people were amazed nothing happened to us.

On the other side of our village was another mountain range. Ole climbed that mountain with Ababa as well. While climbing that one, they ran out of water. They came to a village and inquired if they had some clean water to drink. The villagers told Ole and Ababa to go to a certain hut down the path a way. When they got there, they found that it had Coca-Cola. There were no roads near that place, and it was very remote. Yet Coca-Cola had been there, and no missionaries had ever been there. That impacted Ole as far as understanding the need for getting the Gospel out.

The Sidebottoms traveled five weeks to Ethiopia by ship. They were on a freighter that stopped in Morocco, Egypt, Jordan, and Djibouti on the way. They arrived in Addis Ababa on April 4, 1963. When they first arrived in Kombolcha, they lived in a mud house with a tin roof. They dealt with bedbugs and fleas everywhere. When they turned the lights out, the bugs came out. When the lights were turned on, the bugs disappeared into the dirt walls. It took some time to get rid of most of them, including the rats. They moved to the mission station when they built another house made of flat tin for the outside walls with a wooden floor about two feet off the ground. The inside walls were made of wood, and it was very comfortable.

Although their kids were a little older than me, it was fun having them around. We played in the yard together. One time, Rhonda was playing keep-away-from-her-brother-Michael. She had gotten his white sailor's hat, and he wanted it back. He was chasing her around the yard, and I heard her yelling. I went over there, and she threw the hat to me and said, "Go hide it so he can't get it." Well, I went and threw it down the outhouse hole. That was the end of that game. Michael was mad about losing his favorite hat.

The Sidebottoms were a blessing to the ministry in Kombolcha. They worked with Dad in the church, reaching out to the villages and helping with the correspondence school we now had. They sent material all over the country for people to read, answer questions, and send back. If they sent it back showing their work, they got the next lesson. After a few years, the Sidebottoms moved to Addis in order to start their Bible institute.

Don did a lot of teaching and had a unique way to make the Bible plain and simple for the Ethiopians to understand. He had a way of connecting with the people. The Institute was held in the student center in Addis that the BBFI had. The Sidebottoms lived in Kombolcha for five years. Kombolcha was considered home to them with so many good memories.

The Stampers also lived on the mission station in Kombolcha. They once watched the station and the ministry while we were on furlough. There were a few months' overlap before we left when we were there together. We had Christmas together during those months. It was the hot time of the year, but we still had a fire going and cooked hotdogs on the fire with the doors and windows open.

Tina was five years old when the Stampers came to our station. She would sit on their back steps and talk while Mrs. Stamper was cooking breakfast. They invited her in to eat, but she said Mom would not allow her. Then a few days later, she entered when invited but did not eat. Over the next few days, they asked her about eating a piece of toast, and she said, "No, Mom won't let me." Then a few days later, she was eating breakfast with them. One day, she was caught by Mom, who couldn't believe it because she had already eaten breakfast at our house.

Doug Stamper became a good friend, and we spent a lot of time playing with our Ethiopian friends. The Stampers became close friends through the years. My parents helped them make the adjustments to live in Ethiopia.

My dad had a cow that became like his personal family pet. He bought it from a nomad in Robi. He tied it up and laid it down in the Land Rover and took it home. As it grew up, it followed Dad everywhere. Sometimes it kicked me when I came out of the outhouse. It seemed as if it watched me go in there and knew to wait for me to come out. I guess it was like a game to it. Well, it came time to kill it, but Dad couldn't do it, so he asked Joel Donahoe to do it. Dad couldn't watch, so he went behind the barn. Joel shot it once. Then twice. Then three times. Dad went out and said, "What is going on?" It was still standing up. Joel kept trying to shoot it between the eyes but would miss and shoot it in the nose. Finally, it dropped dead.

Once a year, Buhe (Boo-hey) came along. For four weeks in August, the people celebrate an event with its origins in the Ethiopian Orthodox Church. It marks the transfiguration of Jesus on Mount Tabor. It is the commemoration of Jesus appearing in a supernatural light. Buhe is also a tradition where young people are reminded to value older generations. This event also marks the last days of the rainy season. They celebrate Buhe with very interesting activities.

The boys crack a whip made of braided sisal. The meaning of the whip being cracked is to imitate the sound of the thunder that was heard in the sky. The local people would bake a certain kind of bread. That bread signifies the fact that mothers took bread to their shepherd boys who stayed out late because they thought it was still daylight, but it was Christ's supernatural appearance.

This event occurred during the summer when we were home from school. My Ethiopian friends made whips that they would braid by hand and connect to a wooden handle. They would crack these whips, and the noise would echo all throughout the valley and mountains. They made them for kids and for adults. I usually had one made for me too.

One of the activities with this event was whip fighting. They held a cane in one hand and wrapped their "shumma" (shuh-mah) or small blanket around the arm and hand holding the cane. That club was to block the whip of the other person they were fighting. They tried to whip the other person. Most of the time, they covered their head and legs too.

It was an exciting day when the people on the other side of the river crossed over to fight our side of the river. It was an all-day event. There was a part of the river that had a flat area on our side of the water. About one hundred yards from the river on our side of the flat area, the ground rose like an amphitheater. When the day came for this fight between the two sides of the river, we all gathered on the hills to watch. They would send one guy to fight one guy from our side. Then a few others would join in. After a few hours, there would be many fighting one another.

One time, the other side overpowered our guys and chased them up the hills all the way to our mission station. When that happened, we all ran from them. They even whipped the spectators that they caught. I noticed they were running past me and whipped the others. I was told later that they did not want to whip the "white kid." Thank the Lord for that.

They usually made me a whip every year. I would crack it to make the loud noise. There were a few fights I got in with other boys. I have scars on my back from those few fights. Eric got in fights on occasion too. On time, he came home after being in a fight between our village and another village. He had been hit in the head, and the whip caught him on the side of his head by both eyes and his nose as it wrapped around his head. He was blessed it didn't hit his eyes.

I remember one year when our village had challenged the nearby town to a fight. It was going to be at night. Since most of the people in our village and the town knew one another, they wanted it at night so they couldn't tell who they were fighting. My friends who were going to be fighting suggested I take a flashlight. That way, if we started losing, I could shine the light on the opponents and reveal who they were; then the opponents would stop. Our side could then whip them and gain the advantage. I thought it was a great idea.

We got to the fight, and it began. Sure enough, our side started to lose, so I shone the flashlight on a few of them, and they paused and ran back. Our guys gained the advantage. However, it only made the town guys upset, and they began to get the advantage back and ended up chasing us most of the way back to the village. After we got back, we met in the middle of some huts where there was a small fire. We stood there by the fire and just laughed about what had happened.

We had a small deer come to our mission station. It was a lot of fun to play with, and it was like a pet to us. It was a miniature deer that stood fourteen inches high. This type of deer is called a dik-dik. Jacque liked it a lot. She chased it, and then suddenly it would stop, and Jacque would trip over it. You could hold it, and it sometimes came into the house. It loved to eat cookies. The deer became quite domesticated. It roamed the station freely. After a while, it no longer came around. There was a common footpath next to our fence that many people used to go to the river or town during the daytime. We think someone caught it and took it.

Ole built a little house with bamboo walls and a tin roof. It was big enough for one person. Ole had a cloth door that Jacque sewed that had a string he could pull to raise it or lower it. She remembers sewing that with me sitting next to her. She was babysitting me while sewing. After a little while, she realized as she pulled the needle through she was poking me in the head. I never made a sound. Ole told me I was never allowed to go into his house. Eric had one also near the banana trees down in the garden area. He never let me in his either. One time, a man wanted to get into Ole's little house. Ole kept telling him in Amharic, "Heed, heed!" which meant, "Go, go!" Dad heard him saying this to the man, and he called Ole over and told him to get into the house. Ole got a spanking. Dad said, "We are not here to tell these people to go. We are here to tell them to come!" I don't think Dad saw what was going on and just heard Ole telling the man to go.

My dad told Jacque she had to be careful doing things around the station and not offend people since she was a girl. When riding a horse, she had to wear pajama bottoms (pants) under her dress to cover her legs. Dad built a swimming pool out of cinder blocks for us boys. He cut a barrel in half to be troughs for water and feeding animals. We could use those barrel halves as boats in the pool. It was a lot of fun. Jacque was not allowed to swim because of being in a swimsuit. She got to clean the pool out when it got dirty with all the tadpoles and such. It was not much fun for her.

Ole and Eric liked to shoot their pellet guns at things. They set tin cans on the fence posts and shot at them. Once, Eric put the cans upside down over the top of the poles. When Ole shot the can, instead of knocking it off the fence pole, the pellet came straight back and hit Ole right in the tear duct. Ole chased Eric, who started screaming and running to Mom. His eye teared for quite a while.

They shot a lot of small animals and birds. Sometimes Eric would shoot at the clay pots the ladies used to transport water. If Dad had ever found out, Eric's bum would have been beaten. Once, Eric shot a big crane. It was like an albatross with a wingspan of ten feet.

In those first years, there was a lot of traveling between the mission stations of Robi and Kombolcha. There were some new mission stations started in between. My dad spent a lot of the time building these for the other missionaries. He was probably gone from Mom and our station the equivalent of about two years out of those first four years. He was gone a lot. When he was around our place, Eric followed Dad everywhere and watched him work. He was always by Dad's side.

Just before leaving for furlough, our parents called us into their bedroom to tell us that Mom was going to have another baby. I was in the first grade. They said her name was going to be Kristina Marie.

CHAPTER EIGHT

Traveling the Road North

M r. Cain had a yellow International Harvester panel truck. It was an early '50s model. You had to crank it to start it. Mr. Cain wanted to give it to Dad who said, "No, I must pay for it." It had a lot of miles on it and had been used previously by many missionaries. Ultimately, they agreed on $400, which was kind of hard to pay since our monthly support was $500 a month. It was like a large SUV. This was good for carrying supplies and carrying the family back and forth to boarding school.

The truck had two individual front seats. It only had two doors. To get into the second row (a bench seat), you had to push a front seat forward. Each front seat would tilt forward to allow people to squeeze past it to get into the back. Sometimes we drove it through fields looking for stones to use for building. These fields often had tall grass. There was a prison nearby the town of Robi. They took the prisoners out to cut down trees for firewood. Sometimes they cut a tree but left a stump one or two feet high.

One time, Eric and an Ethiopian helper, Emom (Ee-mom), were sitting in the back seat. Mom was in the front passenger seat. Dad was driving through a field looking for rocks. Suddenly, the front axle hit one of those tree stumps. That brought the truck to an abrupt halt. Emom fell forward and hit Mom's seat with full force. It tilted forward and pushed Mom into the windshield, which cracked and broke. It cut my mom's face in several places, and some were deep cuts. Eric got stuck between the two seats, and Dad had to pry him out. Part of Mussolini pass, which had a long tunnel, had caved in at that time, and traffic was not able to get through to Addis. This delayed them from being able to get Mom to a hospital. They had to wait for several days until they could pass through the tunnel. Dad did all he could from his training as a fireman. He knew they needed to get her to the capital city quickly for a tetanus shot and to mend the cuts. Finally, they made it to a doctor in Addis, and she got the shot, and her face doctored up. In time, she healed very well, and it was almost impossible to see the scars left behind. In fact, if you didn't know this had happened to her, you would never know. Thank the Lord!

One night, when Dad was on his way back from Robi with his helper Emom, the truck stopped running for some reason. They were in an area where the Oromo tribe lived. Emom was of a different tribe, and he was afraid of the Oromo warriors. The truck was full of supplies but just the two of them. Emom said, "It is very dangerous to remain here. These people could come out here and hurt us or kill us or take the truck with all the supplies." It was a heavy-metal vehicle. Emom said to Dad, "You get in, and I will push the truck to push start it." Dad said, "You can't push this by yourself. It is much too heavy." Well, he wanted to try, and so Dad went along with the idea. Amazingly, Emom did get it moving only by the adrenaline of the fear he was experiencing. He got it going fast enough to push start it, and they made it back to Kombolcha safely. Many times, they had to push start that truck, and it always took several men to be able to get it moving. Not this time.

My parents later purchased a Volkswagen pickup. Eastside Baptist Church in Denver paid for most of it. It cost $600. It was not adequate for the job, but they worked it to death. When Dad took Mom and the three kids somewhere, they all sat in the front seat. Ole would sit between Dad and the door. If they ever came upon a policeman, they would have some of the kids duck down so they wouldn't be seen. It was very tight. This pickup was really handy. It was good for carrying supplies and tools for Dad. He used it to carry them to his different building projects from mission station to mission station.

One day, Dad and some of the men were working on the church in Kombolcha and needed more water for the project. They got in the VW pickup heading back down the road for about a mile toward the river. They were moving along at about thirty miles per hour when they passed the entrance to our mission station. One of the workers in the back realized they didn't have any buckets to bail the water out of the river to fill up the barrel. So while they were driving down the road, he decided to step out of the truck to walk to the station and pick up a bucket. When he stepped out, he hit the ground hard and started rolling down the road behind the moving car. Dad saw him in the rearview mirror and immediately stopped. They got out to help him. He told Dad he stepped out because he needed to get a bucket. Fortunately, he did not break any bones and was just skinned up a little. Dad gave him the rest of the day off to go home and recover. He didn't understand the concept of a moving vehicle and what would happen when you stepped out while it was moving.

After the VW pickup, Dad had a chance to get a new Land Rover. We really needed a dependable hard-working vehicle, so Dad wrote Dr. Vick about helping with the purchase. Dr. Vick wrote back and told Dad they would pay half of the $1,600, but that Dad needed to get the rest from other churches. Other churches did give, and we bought it new. I remember Dad pulling up in our new Land Rover Defender. It was the usual basic green color with the long wheel base. It had four doors on the side and an area in the back to carry things. That was an exciting day!

Land Rovers were good workhorses, could withstand the bad roads, and were easy to work on. They had parts available for them, which was important in Ethiopia. It was rated to carry three quarters of a ton. I know we carried loads much heavier than that. We transported supplies to building projects and brought supplies back to our mission station from Addis Ababa. We carried everything inside from dirt to bags of cement, from people to animals, and food to luggage. On top, we would carry lumber, gas cans, barrels, building materials such as tin, and so many other things. In fact, Dad would say there were times we carried three quarters of a ton inside and three quarters of a ton on top at the same time. These heavy loads led to some breakdowns. This car lasted fifteen years. It could do things and go places that our other vehicles were not able to do.

We lived on the road that went north from Addis Ababa to Assab (Ah-sahb) on the coast of the Red Sea and then to Asmara (Oz-mah-rah). These towns are in Eritrea today, but when we lived there, Eritrea was the northern province of Ethiopia. Mission stations were set up in small towns or villages along this road. As you traveled north, you first came to Robi. Then the Hokanson's station was next followed by the one where the Singletons lived and worked. The Powells were a little past them in a place called Jaraniro. They were only there for one term, and then the Yarnells moved there. After that, you came to our station at Kombolcha. Then up in the mountains past Dessi, the Brooks were at Haik. The next station was another hour or two north in the town called Sirinka (Sah-rink-ah). That is the station that the Pierceys started. The last one was Weldiya (Wall-dee-yah) where the Herrings lived.

The Italian-Ethiopian war occurred in the late 1930s. Italy won and occupied Ethiopia for five years. Mussolini wanted Ethiopia as a breadbasket for his country because they grew a lot of grain and corn. Ethiopia was called the Tibet of Africa because it is very mountainous and fertile. There were practically no roads before the Italians came besides a couple of main roads going out from the capital city, Addis Ababa.

The Italians helped to build more roads and especially the main road north. It was a dirt road and had a lot of dust. Most of the twelve-hour drive consisted of white dust. We shut all the vents and windows when we got behind trucks or when vehicles came from the other direction. It still somehow made it into the car. Mom's black hair was always gray or white when we finished the trip. Sometimes you could hardly see because the dust was so thick. I was always impressed with Dad and his skill to drive on that road.

The Italians built a tunnel at eleven thousand feet elevation that we had to go through. Usually, it was quite foggy up there and cold. It was called Mussolini Pass. When you came out of the tunnel going north, you could see for many miles to the lowlands. The road was very winding through those mountains. Trucks traveled this road to carry goods from the Red Sea to the central and south part of Ethiopia and back.

There was a neat place on top of the plateau a couple of hours outside of Addis just before reaching Mussolini Pass. We called it Needle's Eye. It was a narrow gap in the mountains through which you could see the fields, forests, and villages thousands of feet below. If we had time on the trip, we stopped and ran up the sides of the mountains to get a look over the edge to the land below. Some of the hills we climbed were scary because it was so high with complete drop-offs.

Normally, there were kids selling different things that they had made by hand. They liked to watch us run around. We had to be a little careful because there were oftentimes monkeys and baboons. They usually ran from us, but sometimes they would make their noises and show their teeth as if to say, "Close enough, this is our place." If we threw rocks at them, they would throw rocks back at us.

When we reached the tunnel, that signaled to us we were getting ready to reach the town of Debra Sina on the other side and then begin the descent to the lowlands. The tunnel was not very wide and usually only one vehicle could go through at a time.

We would drive through the town of Debra Sina and continue down the switchback roads descending the escarpment. After getting to the bottom, we crossed over a river and then reached the small town and community of Robi. Ole tells a story of when we were near Debra Sina. As we were driving down the road, a deer approached running quite fast and ran right under the car and out the other side. There were a lot of amazing things we experienced on this road.

There was one area in the lowlands where there was a pretty good-sized swamp. Sometimes we stopped there to fish for catfish. Dad told us to go catch our own bait like crickets and other bugs, so we looked under the rocks or anywhere we could to find some live insects for bait. It worked, and we usually caught some fish. That was always fun.

Every missionary who traveled up and down this main road to the north has so many stories of car issues and tire problems. Some had tires come off while driving down the road, and the tire would roll down the mountainside. They had to stop for a couple of hours to retrieve it. It was also inevitable that you were going to run over a few chickens on your trip. Ole went with Jerry Piercey once to Addis from Robi, and they were going fast to get there quickly. They hit at least three dogs and who knows how many chickens. Lyle Yarnell carried a lot of supplies on his Land Rover. One time, he had cement bags inside, boards on top, and pipes tied underneath from axle to axle. He did this so that he didn't have to make multiple trips.

The Sidebottoms had to fix a hole in their gas line with a Band-Aid. Once their fan belt broke, and they didn't have a spare one. They used Phyllis's nylons as the belt. It was good enough to get them to the next mission station.

Several times, we spent the night on this road because something on the Land Rover had broken. Dad was good to have spare parts and spare tires. The dirt road ate up the tires. Sometimes, though, it would be a major problem, like the time one of our leaf springs on the back-left suspension broke. We did not have a spare spring for that, so Dad had to catch a ride on a truck heading to Addis Ababa. Then he caught a ride back with the parts. We had to spend two nights on the side of the road. In the daytime, it was not as dangerous. It was bad when trucks or cars went by, and all the dust would come all over us. But at night, my mind would imagine all the tribal warriors and bandits that were watching us, and at any moment, they would be attacking. It was kind of scary for me as a little boy, especially because it was pitch-dark, and we were out in the middle of nowhere.

One time we were driving down the road, and the car suddenly kind of dipped in the back left. We heard this scraping noise, and Dad slowed the car down. We saw our back tire passing us. Dad stopped the car. The wheel had come off, and the brake parts had flown all over. Next to the road at that spot were some men digging a ditch. Some of the brake parts had fallen into the ditch. We asked for them, and they would not give them back. We kept trying to talk and explain they could not do anything with them, but that we needed the parts. They never would give them up. So we stayed in the car while Dad caught a ride to the next mission station. Mr. Hockenson came back with him, and they managed to piece things back together using nails, pins, and such. When we drove, that wheel had no brakes. They put a nail in the brake line to keep the fluid in. For quite a while, we couldn't get the brakes on that wheel fixed because there was a shortage of brake parts. The time soon came to get the annual vehicle inspection, so when Dad was in Addis, he took the car to get inspected. The brake was still not fixed, so it only had three wheels with working brakes. They tested and looked the car over. They did a drive test to test the brakes. You had to drive down a dirt road and put the brakes on to see if the car responded correctly. They said, "This one wheel on the left rear doesn't seem to hold well." Dad said that he would get it checked after the inspection. They said, "Okay." And it passed the inspection. That was a miracle because they could have not passed it and told him he could not drive it until it was repaired.

Once we were carrying many bags of cement in the back, probably more than the three quarters of a ton allowed. We were going down the mountain from Dessi on the switchback roads that had many drop-off cliffs. Suddenly, we heard a dragging noise and then saw the back tire rolling down the road and then went over the edge hundreds of feet below. Dad had one of the Ethiopians who was with us fetch the tire, and they got it back on. It bent up the back fender, however. Dad fixed it with body putty. The putty was gray, and Dad never did get it painted to match the green. It became an identification marker for our car.

Animals were constantly on the road while being herded by their shepherds. There would be goats, sheep, camels, or cows. One time, we were just past a town called Karikori (Kah-ree-koh-ree) where the road went through many hills and over bridges. We were approaching a bridge when a cow came running. Our front right fender hit the cow and knocked it off the bridge. The owner and other people came running out to the road, all upset. Soon, the local police came and took Dad to the police headquarters and chief's office. He tried to explain it was not our fault, and the animals were not properly watched. The arguing went back and forth and went on for hours. They said, "If you will pay for the cow, we will let you go." Finally, Dad agreed. He wanted to take the cow for the meat, but there was no way to carry it or keep it cold. So, in the end, they got the meat from the cow and the money. It tore up our right-front fender. It was easier to just replace the fender instead of trying to repair it, but we could only get a dark-green fender instead of light-green like the rest of the car. It became another identification marker for our vehicle.

Another time, we had a man walk into the side of the Land Rover. We had gone to Dessi again for supplies and to visit some missionaries. We were driving through town with the slow-moving traffic. There were many people walking on both sides of the road. Unexpectedly, a man walked right into the side of the car. We ran over his feet, and he hit his head and face on the side of the car. People started to gather around, getting all excited. Dad stopped and got out. I remember being afraid of the crowd gathering and hoping Dad wouldn't get hurt. Well, the man was drunk when he walked into the side of the car, and it knocked him down. When he hit the ground, the fall knocked his two front teeth out as he fell face first. Dad put him in the back of the car and drove to the government hospital. They doctored up his wounds. They said we had to help with the expense for the hospital as he needed to stay overnight. It cost $50.

There were a couple of things I enjoyed about traveling along this main road. First, my parents would get me a box of cereal called Alpha-Bits for the trip. The trip was twelve hours long or sometimes more, and one box had to last the whole way. They sure were good, and I would figure just how much I could eat between each mission station or town to make it last the whole way. The second thing I loved was giving out tracts. However, it was done differently. We did not have much time to stop since we wanted to reach our destination before dark. So we would slow down and hold tracts in our hands outside our windows so the people in towns and villages could see them. As we passed by, we let them go. It was fun to see the people run to get them and stand there reading them. I often saw grown men pushing the kids out of the way to get those tracts.

I remember praying and hoping they understood what they were reading. I knew that we were planning to have mission stations and churches all along the road, and I hoped that one day they would hear the gospel. I thought it would be neat if one day a person came to a mission station and said that they had read a tract tossed out of a vehicle and trusted in Jesus. Mom talked about that often to me as I would ask about people not hearing the gospel. Eighty percent of the people lived more than thirty miles from a road. So I asked, "What about those who are not along this road?" Mom explained that is why we need more missionaries and that our churches were sending more to help reach them. She told me that is why our missionaries ride horses and mules out into the mountains to all those villages. It just seemed so overwhelming to me to think of trying to reach all those people.

For entertainment and to help pass the time, we made propellers out of paper with a nail punched through the middle. As we drove down the road, we held those out the windows and watched them spin. If we had time to prepare them before the trip, we colored them with neat designs.

For our trips on this road, Mom made food ahead of time to eat along the way. We stopped for picnics alongside the road or pulled off a little bit. We tried to find a place where there would not be too many people, so we could eat in peace. It seemed like no matter where we stopped, some people would come out of the woods and stand around and watch us. For many of them, we were the first foreigners they had seen.

We traveled this road for 220 miles north of the capital city to reach our town of Kombolcha. The fastest you could travel on the road and be safe was sixty kilometers per hour (about thirty-seven miles per hour). It was just two lanes wide, one each way. There were a lot of rocks on the dirt road. When you got behind a truck, it was hard to pass because of the dust, and you couldn't see ahead very well. Eventually, you could pass. You could hear the rocks being picked up by our tires hitting underneath our car. Sometimes, rocks thrown by the tires of other cars hit our car too.

One time, we were traveling with the Donahoes going from Robi to Kombolcha. It was about a four-hour trip. It was dusk and getting dark. We got behind a tractor pulling a trailer full of farm workers. There was a lot of dust, and it was hard to see. Dad decided to pass to get out of the dust. Just as he started pulling out, a large truck was coming the other way. Dad barely got it pulled back. That was a close call, for sure. We were all so thankful for God's protection. We could have been injured if not killed.

Another time, Mom and Dad were taking us back to school. We always carried two spare tires. They were carried on the roof rack. On that particular trip, we had three flats. We had already replaced the first flat tire and had made our way up the mountains and passed through the tunnel, then we had our second flat tire. After fixing it, we continued our trip. We were out in the middle of nowhere, hours away from the capital city when we had the third flat. We weren't sure what to do. There was nowhere to get the tires repaired. After a while, an Ethiopian man in a pickup truck came along and he stopped to see what our problem was. He thought about our need and then said, "I think my spare tire will fit on your Land Rover. I will give it to you, and when you get to the capital city, Addis Ababa, and you get your tires fixed, you return the tire to me. Here is my address." We had never met the man before. Dad agreed and put his tire on. It did fit well, and we continued our journey for about one and a half hours to a small town called Debra Berhan. It was about another hour and a half from there to Addis. In Debra Berhan, we got our tires fixed. The next day in Addis, we returned the tire to the man. Dad says it was a miracle of the Lord.

One time, Dad was taking the cement mixer on a trailer, going south toward Robi from Kombolcha. We were near the town called Karikori, and the wheels locked up on the trailer. Dad was stuck on the side of the road again. However, there was a small Agip gas station nearby. He pulled the trailer to the station. It was not open, and it was getting dark. Dad ended up sleeping in the car that night. The next day, he got to looking and noticed there was not enough oil in the differential of the axle, which caused it to freeze up. He took it apart, put oil in it, got it working again, and got on down the road to Robi. Again, God blessed and supplied the needs!

We were always excited about making the trip either way. Traveling that road was like an adventure with new experiences every time. We would usually get up around 4:00 a.m. to start the trip. Dad would have spent half the night loading up the car, and off we would go ready to see what was ahead.

A memory that is interesting with the vehicles is carrying Ethiopians in them. Many living in the countryside had never ridden in a car. Most did not know how to open the door or window. It was fun to watch them as they experienced being in a vehicle for the first time. They would just stare outside and watch things pass by.

Sundays were interesting because the people would try to fix themselves up for church or for other special occasions. The ladies in our village would mix butter with spices and smear it in their hair. It was a little rancid and had a unique smell to it. It also made their hair shiny, and they thought that was beautiful. When we were in the car with several ladies, it was kind of smelly. The butter also made their hair discolor with a little tint of green after a few days. When we picked them up in the car, it could be strong. Sometimes they even put this butter on their clothes and then even in their coffee.

When I was in the sixth grade, we made a long trip to Nairobi, Kenya. It took four days and nights to drive there from Addis Ababa. The Sidebottoms and two other people who were teenagers went with us. My parents spent months planning this trip with Don and Phyllis. They calculated and planned the food, water, fuel, tents, and everything else needed. Most of the road was dirt. When we got past the border into Kenya, there was nothing but dry desert, and it looked like the surface of the moon out there. We came across a few Nomads and their camels. We slept in tents near riverbeds and often heard wild animals at night. Ten of us traveled in our Land Rover on this trip. There were three in the front seat, three in the middle seat, and four sitting in the back.

It was an amazing experience, and we got the opportunity to visit with the missionaries in Kenya. Compared to Ethiopia, Kenya was like America to us. We weren't used to all the traffic that we saw in Nairobi, and Dad struggled a little driving in it. We even got sideswiped once in the traffic. They drove on the opposite side of the road in Kenya.

On the way back, we were driving down a dirt road that basically was dirt tracks through hills and valleys. At one point in Ethiopia, we saw a new road they were building, so my dad decided to get off the tracks and get on the new road. To do that, we had to go through a large ditch. While crossing the ditch, our rear-wheels stopped turning. Dad realized we had broken the rear axle because of the load on the axle.

That was very disappointing. However, the vehicle was a four by four, so we put it into four-wheel drive and used the front wheels to pull the vehicle. We got onto the new road, and about two hundred yards ahead, there was a big gap in the road where they were going to put a bridge. That meant we had to get back on the dirt track again. Dad was careful to not break the front axle.

We encountered one additional problem though, and that was going up the hills on the dirt road. The weight of all the people and supplies made the car heavier in the back, so the front tires would just spin on the dirt. We could not get up the hills. Dad said he had an idea. He had most of us get out and sit on the hood to weigh it down for traction. As a kid, that was one of the coolest things. It worked, and whenever we came to another hill, we would all get out and sit on the hood to put more weight on the front wheels. We made it back to Addis Ababa. Of the four days of travel to get back, we had to do this for one day.

God's protection was a sure thing on the roads we traveled throughout Ethiopia and especially the road north. He was there with us every minute, and I am sure we do not know all the ways He protected us from danger and harm. I am certain our guardian angels stayed quite busy as well!

Landrover with heavy load

First Grade Boys - Jon is fourth from right

Family at Bingham Academy

Field Day ribbons

Jacque & Ole with Ole's motorcycle

DC 3 plane we flew in

Jon with friends

Men with block-making machine

Church meeting in school building

Our block house Dad built

School in Kombolcha - 1974

Jon, Eric and Ole after hunting

Jon riding Glory

Negatu & Abarash Wedding

Family picture

Student Center in Addis Ababa

Needle's Eye

Mom teaching to sew

Mom with ladies & project

Baptism in Borkena River

Church in new building in town

One of the trees where Satan is worshipped

Jon with Iyalio and Amino

Tina eating lunch with worker

CHAPTER NINE

How Many Shots?

Living in Ethiopia, we were subjected to a lot of diseases. They were all around us. When we were preparing to go to Ethiopia, we received many vaccines. I am not sure how many vaccinations I have had throughout the years. These were recommended by the US government, physicians, and other mission organizations. Usually, we had to get some shots in our legs because our arms were so full. I do remember dreading every time we would return to the field after furlough because we had to get so many shots. There were times our arms hurt, and we were sick from the side effects of the various shots. We were like human pincushions. As a little kid, these were scary times, and I begged my parents not to have to get them again. We usually got an average of thirteen shots. We got some and then waited a few days to get more until all were received. We spread them out so there was not as much pain. Some lasted six months, and then we had to get them again. Others lasted one year or five years.

There was always the concern of getting some diseases that had not been eradicated in some of those remote areas. There were so many flies, and they would try to land near your eyes and mouth. It was always a concern that we might contract some disease through those flies. Although we did all we could through the vaccinations, with good hygiene and every precaution, we still had to deal with a number of illnesses, from diarrhea to malaria. Many times, when we got sick, we didn't even know what it was. Some of us had malaria. Eric had hepatitis A and B. Jacque and Ole came down with rheumatic fever while in boarding school. They had to be careful so that it did not injure their hearts. Thankfully, they came through that. They were told it could show up again in adulthood. They have never had any trouble after they recovered. Mom and Dad both had typhoid fever. Dad and Jacque both had filariasis, which is a worm in the blood stream usually spread by black flies and mosquitos. Eric had typhoid twice. Mom suffered from sleeping sickness once.

Not only did we rely on vaccinations and observed precautions as much as possible, our main trust was in the Lord. I remember my parents often saying, "So many people are praying for us in America." They said it with confidence as if they really believed it. I believe it was because of the many prayers of so many faithful church members that God helped us through some difficult situations and health problems.

Mom went blind on one occasion when I was a little baby. This blindness came on rapidly. Dad was at a different mission station helping the missionaries build their home. Mom did not have a vehicle to get to a doctor in the town an hour away and had no way to contact Dad. This blindness lasted three days. Her blood pressure went very high during this time, and it also affected how she felt and what she could do. The blindness was so bad that she could barely see me to change my diapers. She became very afraid. There were no other missionaries around, and nobody to help her. She prayed a lot asking God to help.

On the third day of this blindness, Dad arrived home. They immediately left to go up the mountains to Dessi where a missionary doctor was. The doctor listened to what had happened and made his examination. He shook his head and said he did not know why this had happened. With her blood pressure having gone up so high, he didn't think she would ever get her sight back—it might even get worse. This is not what they wanted to hear, and it was a big matter of prayer. They went back home and prayed for God to do a miracle and restore her sight.

The next day, when she got up in the morning, Mom was totally surprised that all her sight had come back. They checked her blood pressure, and it was normal. She felt much better. It was totally amazing and completely of God. You can imagine their joy and praise to God. These answers to prayers strengthened our trust in God and assured us of His care and protection.

When I was five years old, Mom and I were in Kombolcha while Dad was traveling to different mission stations building homes, schools, and churches for new arriving missionaries. One day, I had extreme pain on the right side, and it just kept getting worse. Mom did all she could to help relieve the pain, but to no avail. I began to vomit often throughout the next three days. Mom did not have any way to get me to the hospital to see a doctor. I remember she got on her knees and prayed for me weeping because of the pain I was experiencing, and things she had tried just did not seem to help. After three days, things suddenly began to improve. The vomiting stopped, and the pain subsided. She was not sure what it was all about, and why it all stopped. I remember how she prayed and thanked the Lord out loud for answers to prayers.

Mom said although she never knew personally those praying for our family, she knew they must have been praying because God answered their prayers and relieved me of this terrible pain.

One year later, I was in boarding school in the capital city. My parents were in town to visit us at school and to get supplies for their return to the mission station in Kombolcha. Suddenly, I experienced the same pain on the right side and began to vomit again—just like I did a year prior. They rushed me to the hospital. After a quick examination, the doctors decided on surgery. They said that it was my appendix. When they opened me up, they found the appendix had ruptured, and there were adhesions all over. When my mother explained what had happened a year prior, they were totally amazed that I was still alive. They said that when I was sick the year before, my appendix had ruptured and leaked. They said this should not be, and that I should not be alive. Their explanation was twofold. First, it was God who spared my life. Second, we must have a lot of people praying for us.

I remember going in for the surgery and lying on the bed as they rolled me in. Mom and Dad prayed with me, and then as I was taken into the operating room, I began to cry. There was a big round blue light above me. The doctor said, "Jon, we are going to pray for this surgery." I stopped crying. As soon as he said "Amen," I started crying again. They rubbed a cloth over my forehead, and the next thing I remember is waking up hours later.

When I awoke, my parents were standing beside my bed. It was a strange feeling waking up after surgery. The next day, I was so excited because my parents bought me a brand-new pair of Converse high-top sneakers. They were black and white and looked cool.

When I went back to school, my desk was placed in the middle of everyone else's, and they were not to get near me for a while. I am not sure why, except that there was some concern regarding me getting sick or playing around and my incision opening. I was not allowed to run for several months.

For the next few years, I went to the doctor for tests because I still had issues from the adhesions. My stomach had problems, and I would have all sorts of tests such as lower and upper GI series of tests. I had to drink barium for certain tests, and I remember despising the taste.

For some tests, I had to drink cod liver oil to flush out my system. One time we had gone across the street from the hospital to a small café before having the test. I had to drink cod liver oil, but they would allow me to mix a little Fanta orange soda with it to help me get it down. I always hated the results of this stuff. This particular time, right after I drank it, a nurse came running across the street and told me not to drink anything because their machines had broken down, and they could not do the test that day. I was so disheartened, and I knew what was coming—all for nothing. We did it again a few days later.

There were several health issues Mom personally dealt with. She struggled for a while from lymphatic filariasis, commonly known as elephantiasis. It is a tropical disease. Infection occurs when filarial parasites are transmitted to humans through mosquitoes. Infection can cause hidden damage to the lymphatic system. Her legs swelled up, which is a sign of this disease. This can lead to permanent disability. After a short time, this soon disappeared, and her legs became normal size again, and all the symptoms left. How did that go away without any lingering affects? We can only say it was because of God and people's prayers.

She also dealt with encephalitis, which is inflammation of the brain. Viral infections are the most common cause of the condition. Encephalitis can cause flu-like symptoms, such as fever or severe headache. It can also cause confused thinking, seizures, or problems with senses or movement. Severe cases of encephalitis, while relatively rare, can be life-threatening. Because the course of any single case of encephalitis can be unpredictable, it's important to get a timely diagnosis and treatment. Thankfully, she did not experience a severe case. The doctors diagnosed it quickly and treated it. Again, God watched over her and provided the doctors at the right time and gave them the wisdom to diagnose the disease.

Dad had a couple of injuries. When he was working on the basement of the Donahoe's home in Robi, he was standing on scaffolding about five feet off the ground. The scaffolding broke, and Dad fell suffering a broken ankle. He had to travel to Addis for medical help. He got the bone set, and they put a cast on it. Right away, he went back to Robi to keep working on the house. At night, his foot swelled up because of walking and standing all day long. He was told that he would have major problems in his later years because he did not let it heal properly. He worked too much with it in the cast. He has never had any problems with it, and now at age eighty-eight, it still hasn't bothered him.

One time, Dad and Amaday were building a storage shed. One of the walls was a little out of line and needed to be lined up. Amaday started hitting the end of the wall with a sledge hammer to move it into place. He swung and hit the wall. The head of the sledge hammer flew off, hit the other wall, ricocheted, and hit Dad right between the eyes. It started bleeding a lot. He sat down to keep from falling. He was dazed but soon got up and walked to the pioneer unit where Mom was. He asked her to come out for a minute. She did, and when she saw him, she screamed because of all the blood. She started to panic but soon got hold of herself. She drove Dad an hour up the mountain road to see the doctor. Dad knew how to apply the pressure to keep it from bleeding excessively. He ended up being okay. However, if it had come off and hit him directly instead of ricocheting off the other wall first, it might have killed him. Again, God's protection guarded Dad.

It is so important to pray for missionaries. I have heard stories of missionaries dealing with a certain situation, and God helped them through in miraculous ways. It was later known that a group of people were praying for them at the specific time. I know this happened with my family. I am completely confident that we overcame so many illnesses or avoided some dangerous situations because God heard the prayers of His people on my family's behalf. I wish I could thank them all individually for their faithfulness.

As I have traveled and preached in churches across America, I have met people who have said, "We have prayed for your family for so many years." Do you know what that does for a missionary? It gives confidence and boldness to go on and fully give your life for God, knowing people are going to the Father on your behalf. He hears your prayers. Missionary Randy Perkins (Australia) remembers as a young boy hearing of the missionaries called the Konnerups in Ethiopia. His family prayed for us consistently. Even in remote places, God always had someone there to help or He intervened and healed. There was no doubt that my parents depended on the Lord and the prayers of God's people.

CHAPTER TEN

Protecting Angels

You could say my first experience in Ethiopia was not a pleasant one. I don't remember it, but my sister Jacque does, and so do several missionary ladies. While Mom was quite pregnant with me, she went walking through streets of Addis shopping for supplies with other ladies. They were walking on an uneven sidewalk up a hill when Mom tripped and fell forward directly on her stomach. She was so concerned about what might have happened to her baby. After some tests, her physician said everything seemed to be okay. I know some people would say the doctors got that one wrong!

As a little boy, my hair was very blonde. In fact, when I was five years old I was lying on the front seat of the car with my head in Mom's lap. We were parked near the bank where Dad was doing business. As we waited, two Ethiopian ladies walked by and saw us inside the car. They were surprised to see me lying there. They stopped to discuss whether I was a little boy or an old man with white hair. Mom could understand them and just smiled as they went back and forth trying to decide. They did not know she could understand. After about fifteen minutes of looking and discussing, they finally decided I was an old man, and they walked off, confident that was the truth.

Because my hair was so blonde, even the kids liked to touch my head or even pull on my hair to see if it would come out. It was so different from theirs, and most of the time, they had never seen anyone with hair like it. Walking through the market while shopping for vegetables and fruit was not one of my favorite experiences. I enjoyed seeing the foods all spread out before us, and so many scenes different from what we would see in the United States. What I did not enjoy is the people always touching my hair or white skin. Adults and kids would follow to get the chance. I eventually decided that it was inevitable, and I just endured it.

In addition to their fascination with my blonde hair, the kids I played with found my white skin interesting. A lot of kids would come up to me and touch my arm and then look at their hands to see if the white came off. Some kids would even pinch my skin to see if it reacted, like theirs did. Yes, my skin hurt when someone pinched it. Sometimes people even lifted my shirt up or asked me to lift my shirt up to see if I was white under the shirt too. Over time, this stopped, and when I was in junior high, it rarely happened.

When I was still little and we went to public places, Mom would carry me out of the car. The women would see me and try to spit on me to give their blessings. Mom then tried to discreetly keep me covered so people would not do this. She was always battling with this until I got old enough to walk.

When I was a year old, I fell off the organ seat in our house and broke my collarbone. I was sitting on it pretending to play the pump organ. I was hitting the different notes on the keyboard part of the organ. Suddenly, there was a large earthquake, and I fell off the seat and started crying in so much pain. I cried all night long. This was one of the few times that Mom had a car while Dad was out of town helping another missionary. The next morning, Mom got us into the car and drove through our small town across the bridge, over the river, and then up the switchback mountain road to Dessi. We finally got to a missionary doctor.

He did an examination and took an X-ray of my collarbone and confirmed that it was broken. They put a cast on me that went around both of my shoulders, over my chest, and around my upper back. It made me top-heavy, and it became hard to stand as I was just barely walking age.

Finally, we left the doctor's office and returned home. We drove back down the mountains toward our valley and across the bridge toward our town and village. The bridge over the river was about three stories high. A few hours after arriving home, the bridge completely collapsed from the effects of the large earthquake. Mrs. Sidebottom always said Mom was "one gutsy brave lady to stay at the mission station by herself with Jon while Richard was gone a lot." She said, "You never heard Jeannine complain about anything."

Up the mountains past the city of Dessi was a small town or village called Haik (Hike). This is where Lonnie and Georgine Brooks moved with their family and built their mission station. It was always exciting to be able to go visit them. They were a lot of fun. Their kids were a little older than me. When the Brooks offered to take care of me for about a week while my parents went to another part of Ethiopia, I was excited. I was just a little boy. I don't know why it was, but for some reason, I had this interest in throwing toilet paper down the outhouse hole. It was like throwing streamers. Perhaps I learned it from Eric. Well, the Brooks had this good supply of toilet paper that they had stocked up. It was not easy to get and was not cheap to purchase. I didn't know that, but what I did know is that it was fun to throw it down the long drop.

Georgine Brooks caught me doing that and asked what I was doing. I denied doing anything, and she said I was lying. She was not very happy. I admit that was completely understandable. I knew I was in big trouble and began to run. I didn't want a spanking, so I ran into the house and into the bedroom I was staying in. It had two twin beds. I crawled under one of the beds thinking she would not find me. She chased me into the house, and she knew exactly where I was.

She knelt and spoke nicely to me to coax me out from under the bed. I wasn't buying it and stayed there for a while. Finally, she reached under and pulled me out. She gave me a good spanking. I was very deserving of it.

Lonnie Brooks was Ole's Boy Scout master. However, they were not able to get the material to go through and learn what Boy Scouts learned. The Boy Scouts Club would not send the material requested and said the reason is because they didn't give it to foreigners. Lonnie tried to explain several times that Ole was not a foreigner but an American missionary kid living in Ethiopia. They never did understand, so Ole never got to go through the program.

At least once a year, the local authorities would come to spray DDT in our buildings and in our house. It is a strong insecticide. I remember every year Dad would argue with them that we did not need it. This was done to take care of the mosquitoes and to try to head off malaria. It was also for bedbugs and fleas. They had these pump-like sprayers to apply it all over.

In Ethiopia, the DDT was a white spray and would cover everything with this application. It would be sprayed on the ceilings, walls, and floors. They wanted to spray inside our cupboards where we kept our food, as well as all over our furniture. Their government offices and schools would be sprayed with DDT, which made everything white and smelled bad. Eventually, it would wear off or wash off. They sprayed in their huts and homes too.

The Ethiopians didn't like it either, although they realized the purpose. When they sprayed their mud walls, the bedbugs and fleas would come out of all the cracks in the walls. They said that the DDT was the mother of all fleas and bedbugs. Some of our missionaries didn't have good experiences because government workers forced their way into their houses and sprayed all over.

My dad always argued with them and explained we did not need this done in our home. He explained we had medicine for this and did not need the spray. As a little boy, this was frightening as I watched their discussion. Sometimes they would get angry and demand it. However, every time, Dad could talk them out of it. They never did spray in our home and other buildings. I remember hearing Mom off to the side praying and asking God to intervene and change their hearts. Since they never sprayed in our home, I knew it was because Mom had prayed. I felt that when Mom prayed, God heard.

Christmas was always a favorite time of the year. It was a great family time together when those from boarding school could come home. When we moved into the house made of cement blocks, we got a nice Christmas tree from up near Haik in the mountains. I don't remember having a lot of gifts, but I remember the times we had together. Dad had an 16 mm movie projector with some Abbott and Costello movies, Heckle and Jeckle (a bird cartoon), Geronimo, and a few others. I couldn't wait until I got old enough to run the projector. That didn't happen for many years with Ole, Jacque, and Eric older than me. One of the things we liked to do was eat a bowl of rice with some powdered milk over it. Mom let us put a little cinnamon on top too. That tasted great. We had a great time laughing and talking. Sometimes I laughed so hard and accidently blew the cinnamon right off the top of my rice.

I remember the Christmas I got a bike. That was the best gift of all, and boy did I ride it a lot. We didn't usually get many presents. Mostly it was one nice thing and a few small things in our stockings. We also did a Christmas play for our parents with the Sidebottom kids.

Most of my friends I played with were boys. A few girls would come around and sometimes wanted to play. Most of the time, they were home with their moms doing work around their huts or on their farmland.

One girl would come around often, and we let her play with us. She became a good friend. Her name was Abarash (Ah-bah-rosh), and she was a very nice person. She played cars, tag, soccer and pretty much did everything but shoot my gun. She did not like to go bird hunting with me.

When I was twelve and she was fourteen, I noticed her no longer coming around. I understood a couple of days here and there, but I was home for the summer, and she did not come around at all. I soon found out from my other friends that she could no longer play with us. I asked why. They said because she has been chosen for marriage. I said, "What? She is only fourteen years old!"

They explained that she was not getting married yet, but that she had been given by her parents to the young man who worked with Dad in the church. I couldn't believe it. The girl that we played with was going to get married to the future pastor of the church! Whenever I walked through the village, I often saw her, and she would wave but could never come and play. She now had to learn to cook, wash clothes, go get water, and learn all the things that pertained to being a wife. She could not marry anyone else because a dowry had been paid, and the family made an agreement with the man she would marry. His name was Negatu (Neh-gah-too).

Mr. Cain suggested considering Negatu to help with the church and school because Dad was always helping the other missionaries. Negatu could be the head of the school and the pastor of the new church that Dad started in the tent. Negatu was young and realized he needed a wife. He asked the people to help him. He would say, "I talked to the missionaries, and they said to pray about it." He came to Dad and said, "Everyone is saying to pray about it, and I am tired of just praying about it. I want to see some legs on those prayers."

Negatu wanted Dad to help him find a wife. Dad agreed to help if he could. The SIM had a Bible training time in the summer, so Dad sent Negatu there for two weeks of training. Negatu found a girl who was nice and available, but she was from a different tribal area. He thought that would not work out if he lived way up north, and she lived down south. Negatu asked, "How are we going to work it out to visit the families and get to know each other?" Then Dad went to the Flynns, who were missionaries working in the town of Bati (Bah-tee) which was about forty-five minutes north of Kombolcha. They were with the Brethren Mission from Ireland. John Flynn told Dad that there was a good lady at his church for Negatu. He said, "However, for this idea of them getting together to work, Negatu must come here and preach every Sunday night." Dad said, "But he is pastoring in Kombolcha." Mr. Flynn told Dad it had to be that way to work. They have the Lord's Supper every Sunday night, and they must both participate.

One day, Negatu came and spoke about a girl in one of the classes he taught in our school. He said, "I am going to ask her parents if I can marry her." Negatu went to ask the father of Abarash if he could marry her, but the father said, "No. That is impossible. I have already promised her to a friend of mine." That is the way they did Ethiopian marriages at that time. Even at the age of six, they can have a special ceremony of agreement, and when the daughter reached the age of twelve to thirteen, they would get married. So Negatu gave up on her. But Abarash, who was now fourteen, was impressed with Negatu and told her father, "I will not marry Negatu against your wishes, but I will not marry the other person you want me to marry because I am a believer, and he is not a Christian. So I cannot marry that other man." After several discussions over the following weeks, the father consented to let Negatu marry his daughter. They didn't get married quickly. It all took time to work it out. Even when the father consented, it was not a quick process.

At first, Abarash, as a young girl, didn't know much about how to cook and take care of a home. Negatu, who grew up as an orphan, learned a lot of this and had been living on his own. He taught her how to do those things. She turned out to be a very good wife. She was involved in church and with ladies' meetings. She was a little shy. She became the mother of four wonderful children.

I started my first and only business as a kid in our village. My parents bought supplies of food and things in Addis that came in cans. When we were done with the cans, I collected them and went to sell them in the village. Eric had also done this before me. There were different costs for different sizes. The people liked them to be able to store their grain, beans, cooking oil, or other things in them. They also used the cans to carry water.

Well, I could usually stay up in the village a few hours, and then it would happen. The "Ibd" lady, as they called her, would come. This "crazy" lady seemed to know when I was there. She was demon-possessed and had the voice of a man. My friends often chased her away. Sometimes, though, she would get bold and brave and overcome them to come after me. I remember several times having to leave my cans and run for what seemed like my life. She would be close behind, but as soon as I stepped onto the mission station, she stopped. She never set foot there. I knew all I needed to do was get onto our mission station, and I would be safe. As I grew up and began to understand the spiritual battles we were facing, I came to realize that those demons did not want to come onto the mission station of the Christians. That really impacted my life and helped me understand how the demons fear the Lord and His servants. The power of God became real to me. I learned that God is greater than anything or anyone in the world.

There was another woman we believed was possessed who howled like a hyena. Sometimes we would shine the spotlight out toward the village to see the hyenas. On occasion, we saw this lady walking right in the middle of them. She had to be demon-possessed. You could hear her howling. We saw several people like this through the years.

Our house in Kombolcha was built with a four-foot-high crawl space under it. The door to that space was located on one end of the house. The little door was always kept locked. The barrels we used to ship our personal belongings from the United States were stored down there. Some of our barrels held our clothes. We bought clothes to get us through four years, and Mom had to always guess how fast we would grow. It was always fun to get into our barrels a few times a year. It was like Christmas!

One Friday night, I was feeling sick, so Mom and I stayed home from the midweek service in town. We were in my parent's bedroom reading, and we heard noise under the floor coming from the crawl space. It couldn't be Dad because he was at the prayer service. Who could it be since the door was always locked? Mom was pretty upset about it and was considering going out to see who it was. Then she thought, what if there were several people and what might they do to her? She told me to get down and put my ear to the floor and see if I could hear them talking. I heard several voices and could hear them trying to open the barrels.

I was not able to make out what they were saying, nor could I figure out if the voices belonged to anyone I knew. After some time, Mom started knocking on the floor to notify them that we could hear them, and we knew they were down there. They kept trying to open the metal barrels. What she did seemed not to bother them.

We moved to the kitchen that had a window through which you could see when a car was coming down our little road through the village to the mission station. About thirty minutes later, we saw the lights from Dad's Land Rover coming down the road. When he got near the house, Mom ran out to get his attention and explain what was going on. I was curious to know who it was, so I ran out the door and turned left to run down the side of the house to the back. When I turned the corner to go down the side of the house, there appeared a large white figure. It was about ten feet tall and looked like an angel. It wasn't scary, but it was not what I expected to see. I immediately turned around and ran back into the house.

When Dad got out of the car, he got a shovel and ran to the back to the entrance for the crawl space. When he got there, the door was closed and locked. He opened it and went inside, shining a flashlight. He could tell some of the barrels had been moved. He was not sure if any of them were opened. With the light of his flashlight, he looked into the barrels, and it did not seem that anything was taken. Our conclusion was that they did not know how to take the top off the barrels. I explained to my parents what I saw after running to the side of the house, and Mom believed it was an angel to protect me and keep me from meeting up with whomever it was in the back. To this day, I believe that is very true.

My parents bought me a nice bike to ride around the station and village. The part of the road in front of our village was paved for about fifteen miles each way. I was always adventurous and liked to ride my bike on what would be like a road trip. I always took one of my friends with me. We rode my bike together, or one rode and one ran. We liked to go to a small place called Fontanina (Fonta-nee-nuh). I would tell Mom we were going there, and she always gave me a little money. We took our time having fun and shooting my BB gun at birds on the way. It was basically a downhill ride all the way with a few hills going up.

Fontanina was a small village, but it had a restaurant on the main road, which served the local food and spaghetti. Truck drivers would stop there and eat. We timed our arrival so that we could eat and visit with the truck drivers. Many of them were Italians from the days when the Italians ruled Ethiopia. That is why the restaurant also served spaghetti. The truck drivers always liked to practice their English with me. When we were done eating and visiting, it was time to return home. Usually, the truck drivers were ready to get on their way also.

We asked the drivers if they would take us up the hills to our village. They always agreed and allowed us to put my bike on top of their loads. We either got to ride on top of the loads or sometimes inside the cab of those big Fiat trucks. On occasion, we held on to the side of the trailer while sitting on the bike and let it pull us home. Those trips were always a blast.

There were some Sudan Interior Mission (SIM) missionaries who lived up the mountains near the town of Dessi in a place called Boromeda (Boh-row-may-duh). They had a large leprosarium there. There was a lot of leprosy in that part of Ethiopia. Sometimes we went to visit, and it was a lot of fun to play with the other missionary kids. When we were not in boarding school together, it was fun see them again at their mission station. We had picnics with them and rode on their tractor and trailer like a hayride. They even made a bonfire. The Estelles lived there, and our dads occasionally did things to help each other with vehicle repairs and building projects.

It was a very fertile region, and they had huge gardens. Their vegetables grew to be very large. Some of the carrots were almost as big as me when I was around two years old. Some ears of corn would be twelve inches long. The Sheil family was also in that area. Their dad was a doctor and did some wonderful eye operations to help the local people. Things were primitive, but the missionaries helped in amazing ways. They had cows they milked for the people. They had large fields for gardens, and they grew vegetables for those who were in the leprosarium. Boromeda was over 7,000 feet in altitude in the mountains. Kombolcha was 6,400 feet high.

On the road toward the desert and where the Danakil tribe lived, there was a town called Bati (Bah-tee). It was on the edge of so-called civilization and the wild frontier of the desert. The Irish missionary family, the Flynns, lived there. We got to visit them on occasion. We went to boarding school with the Flynns's son. I remember how primitive they lived out in the "wild," so it seemed. The town had this huge open-air market. The various tribes would come from the desert to trade camels and buy grain and other supplies. Camel caravans brought slabs of salt from near the Red Sea to sell in the market.

I went there on occasion with my parents. I had a little pith helmet that I wore with mosquito netting over it. The netting would be tightened around my neck to keep the flies off my face and out of my eyes. Because of the animals, it seemed there were flies everywhere. They were extremely bad. The flies carried diseases. One of my memories while walking around all the different stalls with vegetables and different foods was the gallows. Every time we went to that market, there were men hanging from the gallows. They had been caught stealing or committing some other crime. Seeing that made a huge impact on me. There were a lot of rough nomadic warriors walking around carrying their guns. That helped me stay close to Dad.

Sometimes we drove down into the desert below Bati to hunt guinea fowl. There were so many in the trees. You could just aim your shotgun toward a tree and shoot. Usually five to seven birds dropped down. They tasted very good. We also chased ostriches in our Land Rover, and as they ran from us, they threw rocks back at the car. It was exciting to see how fast they could go. We only chased them for about forty yards or fifteen to twenty seconds, so we didn't wear them out. On the way to Bati, there was a stream with a very nice flat grassy area under some trees. We stopped there sometimes to have picnics with other missionaries. We sure loved playing barefooted in the nearby stream and climbing in the trees and on the rock formations. I remember vividly those special times together as a family.

One day when I was ten years old, someone brought a baboon on our mission station and turned it loose. It had terrorized the people's animals and destroyed crops, so someone relocated it and let it loose in our station. That baboon was mean. It chased kids back into the classrooms and the workers into various buildings. It chased me into our house. It had a chain tied around its neck that it pulled along. Dad came out of his little office area to see what was going on when he heard all the commotion. When the baboon came toward Dad, it just stood there and sat down. Dad slowly walked over to him and grabbed the chain. He directed the baboon over to a pole and tied the chain to the pole. The school kids slowly came around. My friends said that a man had it as a pet, but he didn't want it anymore because it became a problem to him. They said the baboon's name was Adam.

Well, Adam wasn't a very nice pet. Eric and I could approach it with candy or something to eat. When we gave it to him, we could shake its hand and touch its head. After it got done eating, we could not stay close to it. If we tried, he would raise his upper lip and show us his long sharp teeth. However, when Dad came toward it, the baboon would sit down and submit to him. We never did know why it respected Dad like it did.

After about a week of having it, we decided we needed to get rid of it. Dad had gone to another mission station so Mom, Eric, an Ethiopian friend, and I put Adam into the Land Rover and tied him up in the back. We tried to figure out how to get the chain off, but we couldn't, so we just used it to control and lead him. Eric used a broom to hold him away from us as we coaxed him into the back of the Land Rover. We headed for the mountains.

We got to a remote area where few people lived. We thought it would be a good place for Adam. Again, we looked at the chain but couldn't find a way to get it off, so we opened the back door and tried to coax him out. He wouldn't get out of the car. Eric decided to get into the back with him and push him out. Finally, he jumped out the rear door. However, when he jumped out, he grabbed a wrench. Tools were not easy to come by, and Dad was very careful with them. It was a terrible situation. The baboon was finally out of the car, but he had one of Dad's tools. We couldn't leave him with it.

My Ethiopian friend had an idea. Whenever we gave him candy, he would unwrap the candy and then eat it. My friend had two packs of Juicy Fruit gum. We though if we handed Adam a piece of gum, he would lay the tool down to use both hands to unwrap it, and then we would grab the tool. We tried it. When Eric gave Adam the piece of gum, he placed the tool in his foot to hold. That was not what we expected. We went through both packs of gum, and on the last piece, Adam laid down the tool. My friend quickly grabbed it.

We got into the car and left Adam outside. We started down the dirt road, and he chased us for quite a while. Finally, we got far enough away, and Adam stopped chasing. I am not sure what happened to him. It was a relief he was gone but sad to see him chase us like he didn't want us to leave him in the forest.

Hyenas are ugly scavengers. Their back legs are shorter than their front legs. They have spots on their fur. They have long teeth and very strong jaws. Usually, they find something already dead and eat it. They make an unusual noise as they roam around at night. You rarely see them in the daytime. When they eat something, you hear them making noises that sound like they are laughing. That is why they are known as laughing hyenas.

I remember one time walking at night from the town back to the village with a couple of my friends. There were three of us, and we came upon a pack of hyenas. When hyenas were alone, they would not bother you. When they travelled in a pack, they were bold and might attack. We were very scared when we came across them. We all looked at each other for a split second and took off running toward two nearby huts. When the hyenas heard us, they started chasing to follow us. We got to the first hut and yelled to the people inside. They opened their door, and the three of us ran in. We were shaking. The hyenas stayed around for a while and circled the hut as if they were waiting for us. About an hour later, they were gone and we left to get back to the village and mission station. We walked quite fast and kept our eyes wide open.

We used to hunt hyenas because they killed people's cows or goats and sometimes caught little children. The Wrights moved to our station for a while. Gordon would go out on occasion to shoot a hyena or two that had been bothering the village people and their animals.

It really wasn't in a sporting way, but I guess he enjoyed the way he did it. He would take a jeep out into a field. He put the front window down, which was possible with an older jeep. Then he chained part of a dead sheep to the bumper. The sheep was probably twenty feet or so away. He had a tape recording of hyenas eating and laughing. He played that tape though a loudspeaker. The laughing would draw the hyenas. They came to eat the meat. Two people sat in the front of the jeep with guns and together shot the hyena.

I got to go with him on occasion and watched the whole ordeal. Sometimes it took quite a while until one came. I usually started out excited about the event, but with little action, I easily got tired. When they did kill one, I got to take my BB gun and shoot it after it was dead. No one liked the hyenas. At other times, he would lure them to a tree where he was prepared to shoot them.

I was seven years old and was making a slide out of some boards that Dad had. I had put some saw horses on top of each other and then leaned the boards against them. I tried to make a good slope so it wasn't too steep. Finally, I got it high enough to climb up and then slide down.

I was making this in our backyard near Dad's workshop and little room he had for an office. Dad had looked out at me a couple of times through his office window to see what I was doing.

The last time he looked out, he couldn't believe what he saw, and he ran out as fast as he could. I was hanging off the top corner of the board with my feet off the ground. I had fallen off the side, my chin caught the top corner, my body flung around, and I was hanging. Dad ran and lifted me off the board. I was bleeding profusely. Dad put his hand on my chin and neck veins with a lot of pressure. Mom drove us in the Land Rover up the mountains to the hospital an hour away. When we got there, I had lost a lot of blood. The doctor stitched things up. He said if my Dad had not applied pressure the way he did and at the right spot I would have bled to death. I had cut a main blood vessel. Dad learned some first aid and proper treatment for this type of injury when he was a fireman. Thank God for Dad's experience before becoming a missionary. He used that a lot through our years in Ethiopia.

When I was eight years old, I was riding in a VW Kombi with the Wrights. I had been visiting with them and hanging out with their daughters, Jana and Carla. They were taking us to meet up with my parents. Everyone was getting out of the van through the side sliding door. I was the last one out. Jan Wright was looking to the back of the car and figured we were all out. I was backing out, maneuvering around the seats and was not quite out when she slammed the door shut. My body was out, but my head wasn't, and the door slammed my head between the post and the sliding door. Boy, did that ever hurt! I cried big time, even though I tried not to because of the other kids watching. I always joke, saying because of that incident, my head was squeezed, and it made my nose long.

I don't know why, but I have always been infatuated with matches. Even as a young boy growing up in Africa, I loved to camp out, make fires, and watch the flames. I guess you could say I was and still am a pyromaniac. I was seven years old when I came across a box of matches. Down by the barn on the lower section of our station, we kept some haystacks. These haystacks were to feed our horse and mules whenever they were not taken to the river pasture. They lasted for quite a while and would get quite dry. At this particular time, we had one that had not been used and was about seven feet in diameter and about nine feet tall. It was round in shape and at about six feet high. It started to come together into a point at the top. I had these matches and was wondering how I could make a nice little fire, so I went down to the haystack and took some of the hay in my hand and lit it on fire. It was great, but because it was so dry, it burned up pretty quickly and soon got near my hand. It got hot, and I dropped the hay that was on fire. Unfortunately, it fell onto the side of the haystack, and soon the whole thing was on fire. I remember thinking for a moment how great this was. The flames became huge and started going up high into the sky. Then I thought about Dad. That was a scary thought because now I knew I was in big trouble.

I had been taught that all people were sinners before God, and we stand unrighteous before Him because of our sin. My parents taught that we were born as sinners, and there is none righteous in the world before God—and I knew that was true of me. In fact, no one had to teach us how to be sinners. We are just born that way. That is why we need the Savior, Jesus Christ, who died to take upon Himself our sins. He was righteous but took our sins upon himself on the cross to take the payment of death for us. If we repent of our sins and believe on Him and what He did on the cross for us, our sins are forgiven, and we can stand before God justified with the righteousness of Christ in us. This is really amazing that God would make this way to Him possible through His Son Jesus Christ.

Well, as a little boy, I was, and acted like a sinner. No one had to teach me to disobey my parents. It came naturally. When I began to think of Dad, the burning haystack, and the punishment that was soon to come, I had to plan. I looked around and noticed a man plowing in his field just on the other side of our barbed-wire fence. He had his two oxen pulling a plough, and he walked behind them, directing them to plough each row in his field. My plan came to my mind, and I began to implement it.

I heard one of the workers start yelling loudly that there was a fire, so I ran to the fence and threw the box of matches over by the man plowing his field. Then I ran to the scene of the fire as if I were shocked about it. Teachers and students came running with buckets of water and furiously tried to put it out before it spread across the property and burned any buildings down. Then Dad came running down to the fire looking around. When he saw me, he headed my way. I saw fury in his eyes. He asked me, "Who did this?" Being the sinner I was, I told him, "That man plowing the field did it. See the box of matches over there near him!" Dad did not believe a word I said. He told me to go sit in his office. He helped the rest of the people put out the fire, and soon it was all over.

I waited in Dad's office for what seemed like an eternity. Finally, he came in. He just looked at me. He sat at his desk and wrote on some paper and looked back at me and just stared at me. Oh, this was terrible! He didn't come across as angry, but I could tell he was very disappointed in me. He began to talk about how serious matches are and how dangerous they can be. He spoke about my decision to play with them and how disappointed he was that I burned the haystack down and the money it would cost to replace it. Then he came to the main point. He was disappointed that I lied to him and falsely blamed the farmer. Oh, that one hurt. Then he just looked at me for a while as I bowed my head in shame. I also started to imagine the pain that was soon to come to my backside. After sitting there for well over an hour, as Dad kept writing and occasionally looking over at me, he said, "Jon, I love you, but I am very disappointed in what you have done. Do not play with matches and don't ever do this again. Now, go and lie down on your bed for a while." I escaped the pain of a spanking, but I sure felt the pain of letting him down and the sin I had committed. I knew for sure that day that Dad still loved me, and I never burned down another haystack.

On one of our furloughs, we took a ship from London to New York. It took seven days to go across the north Atlantic Ocean. Ole played shuffle board and won a few contests. The north Atlantic is rough. All of us except Eric got seasick. We would swim in the pool, and at one moment, you would be swimming in the deep end and then abruptly be standing on the bottom of the deep end with very little water as the ship went up and down through the waves. I never went outside during most of the trip because Eric always said he was going to throw me overboard. It was a two-stack ocean liner called the Ss Nieuw Amsterdam.

When I was in the sixth grade, we lived in the student center in Addis for the year. One day, in the back of the building where the cars parked, I was playing basketball. Some Ethiopian teenagers were watching. As I went in for layups, they were trying to mess me up by sticking a tetherball pole in my way. One time they did not get it out of the way in time, and I ran into it hitting my mouth on the pole. It busted my lip and loosened my top left front permanent tooth.

A week later, I was sitting in my sixth-grade classroom. A couple of kids were shooting spitballs through their Bic pens during a break time. I saw one girl point hers at me, and I reacted by ducking. I went down too far and hit my mouth on the edge of my desk. I thought I only busted my lip again, but there was so much pain. I covered my mouth with my hands and ran toward the bathroom. As I ran out, I heard a classmate say, "Look, guys. A rabbit's tooth." When I got to the bathroom, I saw blood and opened my mouth. My loosened top left front tooth had come out. It went through my bottom lip and came all the way out. That's what the boy thought was a rabbit's tooth. The teacher called for help. A nurse came, and Phyllis Sidebottom came. She was at the school that day. They called the SIM dentist, and he said to hurry to his office and keep the tooth warm. Mrs. Sidebottom put it in her armpit to keep it warm and rode with me to the dentist across town. Mom and Dad met me there.

They stuck the tooth back into the hole it came out of. A cast was put over my four front teeth to hold the one in. It was made of pink retainer material, and I had to wear it for one month.

After the month was over, they took off the cast and took an X-ray. Although the root had taken hold, it revealed that bacteria was eating at the root of the tooth because it had been out too long. They had to pull it back out. I went without a front tooth for a while, then they had the plan to put braces on my upper teeth and move all the teeth on the left side forward one position. Once that was done—months later—they filed my tooth down that was now in the front and then put a cap on that tooth to make it match the size of my other front tooth.

This was one of the worst times in my life. It was all so painful. At the same time, I had lice in my hair. I had camped out with my Ethiopian friends and got lice. However, my hair was long, down to my shoulders. I did not want to get it cut, so Mom found this cream to put in my hair to kill the lice. Every night, she washed my hair in kerosene and then picked out the lice. I went to school with cream in my hair, smelling like kerosene and with no front tooth. I didn't have any girlfriends during those days.

One day, we decided to go up to Haik for a picnic. It was the mission station in the mountains where the Brooks lived. They were on furlough, so Dad went to check on things for them. While doing that, we decided to take advantage of the opportunity and have a family picnic. We pulled off the main road and drove down a dirt trail a short way. For some reason, we had a toy doll with us. While we were eating, people walked by and watched us for a while, then went on their way. Two ladies stopped and noticed the doll that was lying there. They talked to each other about it and believed it was a real baby. They didn't know we understood what they were saying. Dad decided to have some fun. He picked up the doll and turned the head all the way around. The ladies started yelling and took off running.

We had many fun times with plenty of laughter, but it took a lot of faith for us to be in Ethiopia. My parents had to trust in God for their all their needs, including clothes, safety, health, education, and protection. It was definitely a life lived by faith.

We were free to do things back then that we would never let our kids do today. We went places that our parents never knew existed and sometimes for days. We went camping with friends and stayed in their huts. If something had happened, they would have never found us. God was always watching over us. So many unexpected things could and did happen. I believe God looked out for us for our parents' sake.

The prayers of God's people are very important, and we saw God's safekeeping, healing, and protection from many dangerous situations so many times in our lives. Only the Lord knows just how the prayers affected the circumstances we encountered. Knowing people are praying keeps the missionary going. We trusted God. He gave wisdom and brought key people our way to get things done—people who were doctors, dentists, and government officials. Knowing people pray for you gives boldness to serve God no matter what. God is good all the time!

CHAPTER ELEVEN

Proclaim Liberty to the Captives

Negatu came on the scene after we had been in Ethiopia a little over one year. Dad needed an evangelist or a pastor because he was needed to go and build for other missionaries and help them. Mr. Cain knew of a young man who was in a SIM orphanage, and he thought that he would be good for our ministry. That young man was Negatu, who was about nineteen years old at that time. He came up to see us and to talk with my parents about the work. He was told we needed somebody to be the administrator of the school but also to preach and pastor at this new church. He said he felt that God wanted him to be an evangelist, so he said, "I'm not interested." Dad said, "Let's pray about it, and you pray and see what God has for you." A few weeks later, Negatu told Mr. Cain that he was willing to come. He was a blessing in so many ways. One important thing was that he could speak Amharic to people in that area. Their Amharic was hard to understand.

Negatu ran the school that eventually had grades one through six. He became a very good pastor for the people. Dad spent a lot of quality time teaching him the Bible and doctrine when he was in town. He didn't get to do much as an evangelist, but he did get to preach at some of the other mission station churches. Negatu was faithful and a hard worker. The people grew to love him and follow him. He was very instrumental in helping my parents start other works and train other leaders in the ministry.

The first church was started in the tent in which my parents originally lived. They put logs inside for the people to sit on. While they were meeting in that tent, Dad was building the first classroom for the school. The size was twenty by thirty feet. It was built out of cement blocks, and the floor was a wooden floor about two feet off the ground. It had wooden steps to go up into the room. When the classroom was finished being built, the church moved from the tent to that classroom. People came to listen, but there were few who responded to the message. Because we did not charge for their kids to come to school, some of the parents came to church out of appreciation, and the relationship building began. They started to like us more, but they did not understand the Bible or the teaching of it. This was all new to them. They listened mainly because we had helped the community with a school, water, and their medical needs. More people came to the church in the classroom than when it was in the tent. Mostly it was the young people who came to church. The older people considered themselves Muslims, and they were instructed not to attend or become a part of it.

Mom and Dad always spoke to the people about Jesus. It would take some time before they came to an understanding of Him and what He did for them. My parents would explain the need for a Savior. The people knew they did wrong things and sinned, but the whole idea was hard for them to grasp. One time, Dad was talking with Ababa, one of the men who worked with him. He had talked to him quite a bit about Jesus. This time, they were standing by the fence. Ababa could not read or write, so they just talked about his spiritual need. They were there talking for a while. After some time, a friend of Ababa's came walking up and looked very serious. He was a friend of Dad's too, and they knew each other well. His name was Husain. Husain heard Dad talking to Ababa about Jesus Christ. He interrupted their conversation and very strongly told Ababa, "If you receive this teaching and leave Islam, I will kill you myself." They were all friends, but this he said with great conviction.

There were a lot of people who lived on the side of the mountain near our village. Most of their sons were shepherds. The girls went out collecting firewood for their mothers to make a fire for cooking. The boys would bring sheep by our station since it was next to the path that led to the common pasture near the river. As they went by our station, they would oftentimes stand and watch us through the fence because we were unusual-looking people to them. The things we did and played with had never been seen before.

One boy who lived on the mountainside heard about the stories and pictures that others experienced during Sunday school. He wanted to come to our station and see these for himself. When he asked his dad if he could, his dad said, "No. Those people will catch you and eat you up!" So he didn't come on to our station out of obedience and probably mostly because of fear.

He soon was old enough to be a shepherd for his father's animals. Whenever Asefa (Ah-seh-fah) brought his animals by our station on the way to the pasture, he would see us out playing, sometimes with other Ethiopian kids. He knew the other kids, and they were never eaten by the missionary. He stood there and watched for quite a while as we played a lot of different games. It was very interesting to him, but he remembered what his dad had told him. He would plead with his dad and tell him none of the others had been eaten. After a while, his dad agreed he could go but to be very watchful and careful.

One day, Ole saw him watching us and motioned him to come and play. Reluctantly, he came but only after the prodding of the other Ethiopian kids. He had so much fun, and we never ate him! He then came to Sunday school, and he heard those stories from the Bible and saw those pictures he had often heard about from his friends. Eventually, Asefa trusted in the Lord as his Savior.

Soon he was being taught about baptism. We did our baptizing down at the river near the pasture where he would take his animals. Those were always fun, exciting days when we baptized. The entire church would leave after the service, and we all walked down about a mile to the river. We would find a calm area that was somewhat deep where a person could be put under the water. We all stood around and watched. After one was baptized and came up out of the water, the believers would start singing in Amharic, "Up from the grave He arose with a mighty triumph over His foes . . ." I will never forget those very meaningful times. When one was finally baptized, it meant a lot, and oftentimes they gave up a lot. At most of the baptism services, Dad baptized the first convert. After that, the local leaders baptized the rest because the government would not give us permission to do so.

When we put up the church sign in town, it was in both English and in Amharic. The actual translation was "Believers of Grace Baptist Church." When the Coptic priest saw the sign and the word *Baptist* on it, he went to the administrator of the town and accused us of baptizing people. They came and told Dad he could not do baptisms. It was part of the restrictions we faced. Foreigners were not allowed to baptize the local people. However, the church authorized Negatu and another church leader, Tesumma (Teh-sum-mah), to do so. When the priest saw that word *Baptist*, he thought people were being invited to be baptized. After explaining things to the authorities, the town leaders ultimately said, "Don't worry. Just keep going on with what you are doing."

Asefa wanted to be baptized, but his parents would not allow it. Dad told him, "We want to be a witness to your family, and the Bible teaches you to honor your father and mother. If we baptize you without permission, they will be angry, and they won't allow us to witness to them. Why don't you live a good life before your parents, be obedient, help them any way you can, and every now and then, ask if you can be baptized." Asefa agreed and started doing that. After one year, Asefa came running to Dad with so much joy and told him, "My father said it is okay now, I can be baptized!" At the next baptismal service, we went down to the river, and Asefa was baptized. Soon after that, his brother, Amaday, was baptized after he got saved. We were never able to reach their father and mother, which is very sad. Many people would not follow Christ, be baptized, or even come to church for fear of what their neighbors would say about them or threaten to do to them. Therefore, most of the people that were reached were thirty years old or younger.

Ababa was eventually led to the Lord by an African-American missionary that was in Ethiopia with the BBFI for a very short time. They struggled living there. When they left the country, Ababa told Dad the missionary had led him to the Lord. Dad said, "Ababa, I have been with you these many years. I have spoken to you very much about Christ, and you never trusted in Him. What was the difference?" Ababa said, "That man spent six hours with me and explained things repeatedly, slowly and very clearly." That missionary talked to people all the time about the Lord.

Near the beginning of our time in Kombolcha, a young man in his late twenties came up to Dad and said, "We know why you are here. We know you are trying to change our religion!" He was quite hostile. But through time, he came to some of our church services and became friendly to us. Although Dad and Mom did things for him to show the love of God, he never came to Christ to our knowledge. He died at a young age during a holiday when he went to town with some Muslim buddies. They began drinking, which was against what Islam teaches, but they did it anyway. They got very drunk, and he got into a fight with the other guys. They ganged up on him and kicked him to death.

We used to have Vacation Bible School down in the pasture by the river where kids were watching their animals. It was always interesting to me that the young boys knew which animals were theirs. Even though they got mixed together in the pasture, they always knew their own animals, and the animals knew their shepherds. For VBS we printed papers with the Bible lessons on them and a page they could color. The national pastor or people from the church would teach the Bible lesson, and then the kids were given a crayon to color the picture. They loved this! They had never seen anything like it before. Adults walking through the pasture from the other side of the river going to town for market saw the kids coloring, and they wanted to do it too. Soon, you could see adult men and women sitting and coloring pictures with the children. They would also stay around and listen to the Bible lesson.

Dad and Negatu decided to have a vacation Bible school. They wanted to have it in the town about a mile away from our village. They rented a storefront building for one week. Many kids attended. The kids had never seen anything like this, and they loved it. It grew in number every day.

After a few days of VBS, Dad and Negatu decided to move our church into town. There were so many more people that we could reach. In town, many of the people were Orthodox or Coptic Christians. So they rented rooms on a more permanent basis. After a few weeks of meeting there, one Sunday the police came and made us close the doors. The Coptic Church priests had complained. They were the state church and had a lot of power. The police said, "You don't have permission to be here in this town." Dad said, "We have permission from the emperor and the crown prince." They said we did not and stood firm and would not let us meet in that building anymore. We had to go back to the mission station.

Dad decided to do more about it than to just take their word. He and Negatu went to see the governor of our province. Outwardly he was friendly, but inwardly he was not happy with us or what we were doing. Sometimes, he made light of our work and wouldn't do anything to help us. They didn't get very far with this man.

Dad then met a young Christian man named Shibaroo (Shi-bah-roo). He worked on the malaria control in our area. He started coming to our church. Shibaroo even went on visitation on Sunday afternoons. He walked up one side of the mountain and down the other, witnessing to people. He became a lifelong friend to our family. He went with Dad to see the governor again. The previous governor was no longer there. He had been transferred. When they met with this new governor, they explained the desire for a church in Kombolcha. Dad told him that we have a letter from the crown prince that gives us permission to preach and teach in this area. He said this letter should be in their files. The governor called in his secretary. She brought the folder with her, and he started thumbing through it real fast until he got to the end. He looked up and said, "No, there's no letter here from the crown prince." Dad got up and went to his desk. The secretary said, "Let me look again," and started going through it a little more slowly. Dad remembered what the letterhead of the crown prince looked like, so he fastened his eyes on that folder looking for a glimpse of the letterhead. Halfway through the folder, he saw it and quickly stuck his finger on the letter to stop the search. The governor didn't have any choice now but to look at it. He read the letter, and he agreed this letter is from his higher official. This man was then open to give us permission to meet and to go to other places to preach and teach. He said to his secretary, "Give these people what they want."

So Dad asked about official permission to go throughout the area. The governor told Dad to write a letter to him and list the names of the other villages to which we wanted to go. Shibaroo helped write this letter and named all the villages and subprovinces around the entire area. When the governor saw our letter, he stamped it and gave complete permission. That governor was there for only two weeks. He said, "This place is so corrupt, I'm not staying." It was evident that the Lord placed him there for that time to get official permission to go into the entire area. What a blessing! They went back to renting a small room in Kombolcha. Dad believes God put that man in that position for such a time as this. The local authorities ended up appreciating the work my parents did with the new school, water project, medical help, and the church. We always had a good relationship with them.

Mo Garner came to visit the missionaries and their work in Ethiopia. He was good a man and a strong preacher. Dad was not sure how he would come across with the Ethiopian people; however, Mo preached in the church one night. It was in the small room of the school, but it was jam-packed with people. They were coming to hear the message but also to see this man from America. At the end of his preaching, six people made professions of faith. That was very unusual but amazing to see. God certainly blessed that service and used Mo Garner in an important time. It was as if that was the catalyst to see things really begin to move forward with the people.

The growth of the church caused Dad and Negatu to find a piece of ground where they could build a permanent building. The problem was that we were not allowed to own any land. Negatu said a couple of other people could buy the land in their name and so they did. Dad never knew who purchased the property. The land was on the side of the main highway going into Kombolcha. It had a steep drop-off down to where the church building would eventually be built.

We made our own cement blocks with a hand machine and the cement mixer. Amaday and others were helping do a lot of the work. The building would be sixty by forty feet in size with classrooms down both sides that you could enter from the auditorium. Dad laid the blocks for the entire building by himself while these men mixed mortar and brought the blocks to him. One day, the cement mixer stopped working and Dad took it to Senior Rosmo to try to fix it. While they were looking at it, Tesumma organized the men, and they mixed the concrete by hand. By the time the mixer was running, the men had most of the concrete mixed by hand and the footing poured. Senior Rosmo made the A-frames from steel at his garage. The building had electricity enabling them to have night services and training sessions.

The church grew quickly. They were excited to see people come to Christ and to finally have a place of their own in which to meet. A good core group of people were trained and served in the church. When we moved to the new building, we were always in need of Sunday school teachers because of the growth. Most of the people at church were new converts. They did not know a lot of the Bible in the beginning. There was one boy who got saved and learned the Bible quickly. Mom worked with him to help him become a Sunday school teacher. Everyone in the community knew him, and he was quite energetic and very popular. At the age of twelve years, when Shewaye (Shi-wah-yee) started teaching Sunday school, many children and even adults wanted to come and hear him. As Shewaye walked to church on Sundays, it was amusing to see kids get behind him and march single file to Sunday school. There could be up to thirty kids following him to hear him tell Bible stories.

The land and the building were down a little hill from the main road in the town. We put a sign on the side of the road. Before Sunday school, I stood by the road and invited the kids to come. I thought I was a part of what my parents were doing and wanted so many kids to hear the stories of the Bible and eventually of what Jesus had done for them. Many kids came. I think most came initially because of this white kid with blonde hair inviting them. Even if they came for that reason, they still got to hear the Gospel.

Mohammed was a young boy around eight years old. He came to know Jesus as his Savior. He was from a Muslim family. Because of his salvation, his father kicked him out of their house, and he had to go live with his uncle. It was hard for him to come to services because his dad still had jobs for him and made him work on Sundays. Sometimes he would sneak out and go to church. When he came home, his brother would beat him and threaten to kill him if he continued going to church. He suffered a lot for Christ and was willing to take that risk even at a young age. He never gave up his faith.

Mom did a lot of work with the ladies. She had a weekly Bible study. However, not only did she teach them from the Bible but she also taught them how to sew and knit. They learned to knit blankets and things that they could use. Mom provided the yarn. They loved this, and it was a favorite time of the week for them. A lot of times, the Bible study was in the homes of the women, particularly after the church moved to town.

My mom also played a key role in teaching the Sunday school teachers. She would spend time training them and then observing them during their class times. She used flannelgraph when telling Bible stories and lessons. We ended up having some well-trained, exciting teachers. The kids loved the stories and seeing the big pictures that went along with them. I used to love to go to the classes and learn too.

Mom also played the piano. We didn't have a piano, but we had a pump organ. It could fold up into a suitcase made from wood. It would fold up into a one-foot-deep-by-four-foot-long box. When it was set up, you could sit at it and play it like today's keyboards. She played it when they sang the English songs and hymns. She taught the people those songs. They mixed the English songs with their local songs in the services. Mom could not play with the local songs. It was very difficult to learn their tunes because they were very different from our music. Jacque also played the pump organ at church when she was home from school. Bugs nested inside the organ and came out when it was played. She could feel those bugs crawling on her legs when she played. Jacque and Ole played instruments for music specials. She played the accordion, and Ole played the clarinet. At first, the people would laugh at them because they had never seen this before. Later, they learned to appreciate it and clap for them.

Mom was known by some of the other missionary wives as the one who helped them adjust to a new life in Africa. Mom had spent a few years there and had seen people come and go. When new missionaries came, she took time to encourage the wives through their adjustments with living and language, showing them where to shop and find the right food for their kids. She gave them a feeling of security. Mom was a great listener, and many knew they could come speak with her and leave encouraged.

Cooking was one of her specialties. Missionaries always enjoyed stopping at our mission station and receiving a great meal. One of the favorites was macaroni with tomatoes and beef. She really did care for others and wanted to make their visit a special experience.

Mom was also known for her humor. It was contagious, and people loved it. Dad's humor is dry, and Mom's was a complement to that. She could be very funny. When crazy, funny things would happen, you would just have to laugh to keep from crying. It was almost like you had to laugh to survive.

Mom always said her main ministry was to her family. Although we were away at school most of the year, she spent time cooking special meals when we were home, making special gift/food packages to send to us at school, and she spent a lot of time praying for us. Dad spent at least two years of their first four years away from Mom and home. No one will ever know what all Mom endured in his absence. However, at no time did she ever complain. We all remember that. Mom prayed constantly for Dad. I remember her reading her Bible a lot, and it was amazing to see her strong, consistent relationship with God.

We were involved in a unique ministry opportunity visiting the villages on the other side of river. It was like visitation at night. In the daytime, the farmers were working in their fields with their crops. At the same time, the kids were watching over their animals or getting firewood. That meant they were only home at night. We had two mules and one horse. The mules were named Glory and Jack. The horse's name was Tony. Tony did not like it if two people rode him, and he would take you under trees to brush you off. In Ethiopia, it was more common to ride mules than horses. The mules were easier to care for and train, and they were more sure-footed. A mule liked to have a horse around. Our mules and the horse were taken to the pasture by the river about a quarter of a mile away from our station every morning. When it was getting dusk and time for the animals to come home, our mules followed the horse that knew where the barn was. If we did not have a horse for them, they would go somewhere else following other animals. That actually did happen a few times. The mules ate most things, including thorn bushes. When riding the mules at night going along the footpaths on mountainside, these mules would sometimes get spooked by a noise. Most of the time, they just stopped but wouldn't run away. Their ears would move around to listen, and eventually, they would move on when ready.

I didn't get to ride very much because we only had two mules. However, one night I was riding on Jack with Shewaye. I was ten years old. Now, Jack was kind of an unpredictable mule, and he liked some people more than others. He liked when Shewaye would ride him. Since Shewaye was riding on Jack, we thought I could ride with him too. That had generally worked well in the past. It just so happened that we were riding along, and Jack got spooked by a hyena's noise. Jack started bucking a lot, and I fell off. Shewaye fell off too because he didn't want me to be alone out there at night with the hyenas. The others came back to see what had happened. Jack kept running for a while, and it took a few hours to find him in the dark. We never did make it to a village that night to teach.

Hyenas were always out at night. They usually did not bother us. Now, if they were in a pack of seven to ten, it could be dangerous. The mules would hear them and stop. We would yell or shoot a gun, and then the hyenas went away. We'd wait until it was clear and then keep going.

Most of the people in the surrounding area and mountains knew of us. Word spread fast about these people from America. They also knew of us because of our school, the water project, and the medicine Dad used to help the people. When we would arrive in their village, they always welcomed us, and several people would come to one person's hut, or we would meet outside. We lit our lantern and taught them. There was always an Ethiopian with us to help interpret or help with problems. Most of the people were Muslims. They could not read or write. Therefore, we also taught the Amharic alphabet and how to read and write.

As I mentioned before, the Sidebottoms joined us in Kombolcha. They became very involved in the church when it was meeting in the school building. Don preached a lot while Dad was gone and Negatu interpreted. They went down to the pasture by the river during the weekdays to teach the shepherd boys Bible stories. Mom and Phyllis taught the children. The kids memorized many verses. They loved to do that. After one hundred verses were learned, they got a Gospel of John. After the next set of verses were memorized, they got a New Testament. Then after the next set, they got an entire Bible. Oh boy, that was a grand prize, and they tried so hard to get that Bible. Sometimes, Mom and Phyllis walked a little over a mile from the village to the town to be seen by the kids and to make contact with the people. The kids would run to get in line and follow them all the way to town to the new church building.

Usually, the next week, the Orthodox priest would go to all the parents and tell them their children would be expelled from school if they went back to those classes on Sunday. Most stopped coming for about a month or so but then later returned because they loved the Sunday school classes so much. Sometimes on Sunday, the priest would walk into the classes at our church during the teaching and would stare at the kids and then leave. It was his way of intimidating them and taking roll of who was there.

On the weekly market day, hundreds of people passed our station as they came from the rural areas to buy and sell. It was heartbreaking to see so many people walk by who desperately needed to hear the gospel. The Sidebottoms decided to go where the people's villages were located throughout the mountain ranges. They rode the mules on footpaths to reach the people. Amaday went to help them and take care of the animals. They would stay out there for five days searching for villages and finding friendly people. They took their cots, sleeping bags, utensils, and food with them and set up camp. They slept in a small tent at night. They used flannelgraph and flash cards to teach. Amaday slept outside the door of the tent or sometimes in a nearby hut if he felt they were safe.

The people were not always welcoming. Once they came to the base of a hill. The people in the village above them at the top of the hill sent messages down, saying, "Don't come up here. We don't want you." So they proceeded to the next village. They did not always feel safe. There was the fear of people trying to steal their mules. At one village, there was an uneasy feeling. They didn't feel safe. It was cold that night, and Amaday slept by the tent door under the saddle blankets. He tied the mules up as closely to him and the tent as he could. Nothing happened that night, but in the morning, he said, "We need to leave. These people are hostile, and I don't feel good about staying here." They later heard that a foreigner had gone through there previously who was a tax collector. The people did not like him or his purpose and ran him off. They were leery of any foreigners and were not kind to them.

There were so many villages in every direction you looked. How were they going to reach them all? The Lord led the Sidebottoms to train national leaders and teachers to go out in greater numbers who would be more accepted. They decided that a Bible training institute was needed to reach the whole country quicker. After a few months, they decided to move to Addis to start this very important training institute.

The Wrights came after the Sidebottoms left to start that Bible institute. Soon, Gordon hired a man to help continue with this village ministry. He hired the man to go to the villages and care for mules. The people in the villages close to us were usually friendly and eager to learn. We had very few problems in these nearby small villages. Our reputation grew from the services we provided to the community. Those villages that were farther away were not as welcoming and more reserved toward our efforts.

People were grateful to learn to read and write. However, they did not respond favorably at first to the teaching of the Bible. The school helped a lot in getting them to trust us. Mostly, the older ones came to school, and the younger ones stayed home and worked. To send a child to school was a new thing for the villagers, but they came to appreciate it. That made it easier for them to go into these villages and be welcomed by their kids who were the students. A few people came to church from this outreach. It was mainly the young teens who came to the church services on Sunday because of being in their homes at night.

The Yarnells also had a ministry reaching out to the surrounding villages by muleback. Lyle Yarnell always seemed like a tough rugged man to me. At first, I was afraid of him. He was known for being able to handle animals, and especially mules. In the United States, he had experience with the rodeo and working with horses and mules. One time, the veterinarian in Kombolcha went to see Lyle at his mission station because a disease was going around, and they needed to vaccinate his mules too. He had a barn that looked like a big hut. They took their mules inside it to get their shots. One mule reacted in fear and started running out of the barn and down the field. Lyle grabbed it by the neck and rode it for about seventy-five feet holding on until it finally stopped. He walked it back to the place in the barn. The Ethiopian vet said, "That is not a man." Lyle's daughters also learned to do a lot with the animals and rode them all over the area.

Yimir was our night guard for many years. He lived on a small piece of land next to our station down below the barn. He had several huts on his small strip of land. He had a few goats and chickens. In the daytime, we could sometimes hear his wife crying and sometimes screaming. It was not normal. When Dad heard about it, he inquired of Yimir as to what was going on. Yimir explained that it happened when he beat his wife. Well, Dad wasn't happy to hear about that. He took some time to explain to Yimir how to love his wife as the mother of his kids. Dad taught him that he should show respect to her and should never beat her. Yimir listened intently and nodded his head in agreement. He said he had never heard any teaching like this, but that he would follow it.

About a month later, he came to speak with Dad. He looked sad and confused. Dad asked him what was the matter. Yimir said his wife had left him and returned to her parent's village. Dad asked why this had happened. Yimir replied, "I followed your teaching, and I have not beat my wife for one month. She left me, and her parents told me she feels that I don't love her anymore because I stopped beating her." There was much to teach these people of the love of Christ and what is true love for one another.

Although our village was near a town, it was still in a remote area. There were villages all around the mountains and valleys. Some people did farming, and others had animals that they kept. A few people worked in the town.

There was a lot of witchcraft in the area. People said they were Muslims, but when difficult things came upon them, like bad health, crop failures, or bad luck, they would go see the witch doctor. I remember seeing people possessed by demons. It was quite prevalent, at least compared to what we would see in America.

Ole's dream was to shoot a baboon and then have its head stuffed with its face snarling. He wanted to put it above the door of his dorm room. He went on a hunt to find some baboons and perhaps shoot one to fulfill his dream. He came across a pack of them. He picked out a mean-looking male and prepared to shoot. He had his aim right on it, and then he noticed a lady sitting among them. He started yelling at her to get out. "Go, go, get away from there!" She slowly walked away, and the baboons ran because of his yelling.

She was demon-possessed. He never did shoot a baboon and ran home to tell Mom and Dad about what he saw.

Yimir's first wife died, and so he went to find another one. He went to another village on the other side of the river and behind the mountain. After a short time, he brought back a new wife.

As soon as they arrived at his house, she began to have some strange problems. He would take her back to her village, and things would go back to normal. Whenever they'd come back to his house, she would have problems. They were problems with demon possession. Demonism was very real. One time when he came back with her, he asked Negatu to come over and help. Negatu went over to his hut and began to speak with the woman. All of a sudden, this demon began to speak through her. According to Negatu, they were talking about this woman, Yimir's wife. It was a male's voice coming out of this woman, and it said, "This woman is my wife," And it would argue that point. We were never sure if later they somehow appeased that demon, or just what happened. People dedicated their children to the devil, and many times, the demons considered that a marriage.

There was a young man who lived in our village. He married a girl from another village. A few days after their wedding, she abruptly couldn't walk normally on her two feet. She could only walk with hands on the ground behind her and stomach facing up. Several weeks passed by, and Dad saw the young man and asked how his wife was doing. The man explained she was doing fine and walking fine. Dad asked what had happened. He said they went to a witch doctor who supposedly appeased that demon, and so it is leaving her alone now.

Our landlord lived about seventy-five yards up the hill from our mission station. His wife would come over sometimes to the station and visit. We had built some tin sheds as living quarters for some of the teachers and workers. One of the workers had married the landlord's daughter. One day, Dad heard some noise going on in one of the tin sheds. It sounded really strange. When he went in, he found the landlord's wife leading that couple and a few others in satanic worship and a séance. Dad chased her off the station and down the road. Although people claimed to be Muslims, they still believed in demons and worshipped them.

Another time, the landlord came over and was carrying a rifle, and extremely mad. Dad was laying blocks on a building. He stopped to greet the landlord. With great anger, the man asked my dad, "What did you do with my wife? You have taken her somewhere. You took her clothes and everything and took them away." Well, Dad realized what he was talking about. She had come to Dad carrying a small wooden box and said she needed a ride to town. He guessed she was leaving him. Dad did not give her a ride. Dad told him he did not know about his trouble. The man finally cooled off and left for town to find her. Dad was not sure if the man was going to shoot him because he was so angry. That was a close one.

The Yarnells lived in a small town called Jaraniro. There they built a mission station. It was a couple of miles off the main road up some hills. When you turned off the main road to take another dirt road up the hills to where they lived, there was a huge tree. The local people believed Satan lived in that tree. You would often see different colors of paper on the branches. Sometimes there was food up in the tree or at the base of the tree. The people would take gifts to the devil at that tree to appease him and keep him from doing harm to them. Water came out near the base of that tree like a spring. Lyle wanted to help the people by providing water, and he built a stone trough for their animals to drink out of. They never did use it because they had set that place aside as the place where Satan lived. The people later tore it down after the missionaries left.

The people in that area lived in great fear of evil spirits. Oh, they were real and were very much a part of their everyday lives. They were scary. Some people were so afraid of the devil, and they believed he liked to steal male children. To keep him confused, they would give all their kids a girl's name until they were twelve years old. When the boy turned twelve, he was given a boy's name.

Once a year, the Muslims and the Orthodox Christians went to the next little town called Fontanina. They claimed that a man who looked like Jesus lived there. At that time, hundreds of people went there for some type of worship only because of this man. There was a grove of trees, and people picked out a tree as the one to which they would bring gifts like food and money, and place them at the base of that tree. This was done to appease the spirits who were very active in their lives. Throughout the year, they would take different-colored cloths and tie those to the branches and place money at the base of their tree. They thought that would make the demons happy. One schoolboy said he used to go there after all the people left. He picked up the money at the base of these trees, and that helped pay for his school fees and books. Many people claimed to be Orthodox Christians, and yet they believed in, and feared, the devil and his demons and did all kinds of things to appease them.

At night in the village, we could hear people chanting and carrying on, making all kinds of scary noises. They did this to make the demons happy. They believed one could not cast out a demon; it could only be appeased. Through gifts to trees, by calling in the witch doctor to chant and do ceremonies and all sorts of other rituals, they tried to make them happy. Sometimes these demons would demand certain colored clothes to be worn by people. They did whatever the demon wanted them to do. Not only was it hard to reach the people with the Gospel because they claimed to be part of another religion, but also because of these fears and beliefs about these demons. It was hard for them to change from the fear of the devil to freedom in Christ, but when they did, it was amazing to see the huge difference in their lives.

In the town of Robi, Dennis Herring saw some crazy things like rocks falling from the inside of a grass-roofed hut. He saw men walk on hot coals in the name of Satan. This was all very real to these people, and they lived in great fear.

People poured oil and butter on a black rock near Jaraniro to appease the evil spirits. They said this was to give them a safe trip to the market and back without any problems. On days when it got real hot, the people made coffee and poured it at the base of a particular tree. They said they were giving thanks to the tree for the shade it provided for them and to ask for help in other ways.

As the years went by, the number of churches grew with each mission station. Not only did we have churches on the stations, but then others were started in the surrounding communities. I remember how some of our churches got together to meet each other on occasion. It was a time of encouragement for them to meet other believers who had come to Jesus. They shared their testimonies with each other. The Brooks occasionally brought their people to visit our church services. These were good times for the believers. This encouraged them as they met believers from other towns and saw how God was working in other areas, and they were not alone.

Some of the churches started volleyball teams. They traveled to the different stations and played each other. It was all in good fun and fellowship, but it did become quite competitive. I was just a little boy, so I couldn't play. However, I sure enjoyed traveling with them and watching them play.

The school was required by the government. However, it was also used to teach about Jesus and the Bible. The people knew this, but they were more concerned that their children learned to read and write, so they would put up with the other. A lot of the families sent one child to school but kept the others home to do chores, like watching the animals or the girls helping to collect firewood and water. When the early missionaries had to start these schools, it seemed more like a hassle, and some didn't understand why the government required them. The missionaries at first weren't happy about it. They were told to teach the people to read and write. Most did not know much about starting and administrating schools. Dad figured we would just teach them to read the Bible and write about it.

As time went by, it became clear how the schools were very beneficial for the ministry. It enabled the missionaries to reach the young people. Sometimes our teaching of the Bible created problems. The parents said they believed in Jesus, but not as the Son of God. He was only a previous prophet. They didn't mind if their children believed in Jesus Christ, but they did not understand what it meant that He was the Savior. When their children wanted to be baptized, that's when the problems came.

Negatu was one of the first teachers, and slowly we added more teachers. Negatu knew some of them and recruited them. Others were sent by the government to teach. The school grew to the point that we had one teacher for each class. It had six full-time teachers and grew to 270 students. A good number of the schoolchildren who came to school also came to church. Many of them accepted the Lord Jesus as their Savior.

It seemed like the devil did a lot of things to make life difficult for the missionaries and their ministries. One time, the government decided it was going to bring taxes upon the missionaries. They said we had to pay the taxes on behalf of those working for us. They knew they would get nothing from the local people themselves, so they would get it from the missionaries. Most of the people with us made only 45 US cents a day. It was still more than what most other people made working other places. My parent's monthly support was $500 a month so we couldn't afford to pay them much.

The new tax for those missionaries in Addis was a more difficult issue because they were close to the main government offices. Denton Collins had to pay $500 a month for their taxes. When missionaries would leave the country for furlough, they couldn't leave unless they had a receipt showing they had paid their taxes. Some hesitated to pay because the government was always changing their minds. Dad told one missionary not to pay and especially not in the capital city. He said perhaps they would eventually drop the tax or change it. Dad went to the authorities in Kombolcha. There they wanted him to pay retroactive, and Dad said he would pay last year's and this year's only. The official agreed. Dad told others to go to small towns to pay because they were more open and willing to give breaks. He never had to pay again. However, those who paid in Addis had to pay for several years. The government stopped this tax after a few years.

Ethiopia was not an easy place to live and serve. These mission stations were spiritual oases in which to stop and visit each other. The missionaries drew close together, and they knew they needed each other. The mental and physical wear and tear was enormous, and knowing others were there to help you through it was a tremendous blessing. We all became like family. We called all the parents aunts and uncles.

The first year, the Donahoes and my family arrived in Ethiopia. In 1963, others started coming, and soon more mission stations were started. Our missionaries also had schools and/or clinics and started churches. From those mission stations, they reached out into the villages and towns throughout the countryside. The SIM mainly had their stations in the south, and this method of building mission stations seemed to be successful. The first station was in Robi located in the Shoa province. Our mission station in Kombolcha was the next one started and it was located in the Wollo province. It was over three hours north of Robi. Then, one hour north of Robi, the Hokensens started a mission station and lived in tin buildings. The next station was about an hour north where the Singletons lived.

At first, they lived in a mud house, but then they had a prefab house brought up by trucks. The next place was Jaraniro that the Powells started. It was very primitive there and not easy to get to. When the Yarnells took over in Jaraniro after the Powells left, they also started a church on the main road in Kemisi. It is at that little town that you turned off to go up the mountainside to Jaraniro. Then you would come to a small town on the main road called Harboo. An evangelist named Tekele (Teh-keh-leh) went there once a week to preach. He also held services for children there. He was sent out of the Kombolcha church. Although around these stations most of the people were Muslims, you did not see any mosques. Some of the people were Coptic Christians, and you could spot a few of their churches here and there.

Then we had one student who started a church in Dessi, which was just north of Kombolcha. That was about one year or so before communism came, then it closed and did not survive. After Dessi was the mission station Haik where the Brooks were. A couple of hours north of Haik was Sarinka (Suh-rink-ah) where the Pierceys lived and worked for a while. Farther north was Weldiya where the Herrings started a mission station.

We became close to the other missionaries. Several of the missionary kids were my age: Danny Donahoe, Andy Brown, Jay Piercey, David Metts, Ron Worley, and Doug Stamper. We had good times whenever we got together either at the different mission stations or in Addis.

My parents trusted the Lord to watch over their kids. They had to. They relied on Him to take care of us both living in the country-side and at school. Mom had a strong relationship with the Lord. Living in a difficult place and dealing with the living conditions as she did only drew her closer to Him. Mom was determined to live for the Lord no matter what things came her way. She wanted to be a good example to her children and be strong for them. Even when she struggled with handling her kids going off to school, we rarely knew that it was affecting her. She was an amazing lady, and she relished the opportunity to serve the Lord as a missionary.

Mom and Dad ministered to the people in all sorts of ways. They showed the love of God and lived a life exemplifying Christ. They helped the people with their sick kids, gave them food, helped with medicine, and mourned their dead with them. Oh, they wanted all people to come to know Jesus. They sacrificed a lot for that to happen and, I believe, at times that included their marriage and their family. It may not have been the best way, but they gave their all to the Lord and His service.

Ministry in Ethiopia was unique. You had the various tribes with their beliefs. You had the different religions with their beliefs. You had a lot of devil worship and the effects of that. Some of the country people could not mentally grasp what was being taught. Some did not like the foreigner bringing a strange message. There were a lot of obstacles to overcome besides just trying to live there.

It became important to train national leaders to reach their own people, so the missionaries would witness and preach while they instructed faithful men and women to do the same. Negatu was the main person in our ministry. He did a lot of the teaching and preaching, being mentored by Dad, Don Sidebottom, and Gordon Wright. Then, with the experience of going to all the villages at night or for up to five days on mules and horses, it became evident more help was needed. They needed more help to reach the entire country for Christ.

The language was hard and different in places we went. We needed help with that too. This is what made the Sidebottoms determined to move to Addis and start the Baptist Bible Institute in the capital city. We needed more help and more leaders. The missionaries could not do it all. The institute was doing well, and leaders were being trained and starting new works. Young people were getting interested in serving the Lord. The missionaries began to see that it was vital to train the people in the churches but also to train leaders to go start new works. They needed to know the Bible and doctrine if the works were to survive and multiply. The teaching needed to be specific and intense so that they could reproduce themselves with their own people.

Many Ethiopians still need to hear of Jesus Christ and the salvation He brings by His death on the cross and His resurrection three days later. They are still blinded by their religious beliefs and the snares of the devil. Many in the countryside still offer their gifts at sacred trees to appease the spirits. They ask the spirits for protection and success. They make vows in return for these blessings. They believe if they don't keep their end, misfortune or sickness will overcome them and their family, or the entire village could suffer. They seek advice from the spirits of their ancestors and pursue their favor. Some of this can be very frightening. They are not always interested in our "foreign" religion. These people are not at peace and are bound to Satan and false beliefs or distant gods. They are captives to the spirits of their ancestors. Spiritual darkness is all around them. They need the love of Jesus, but they are surrounded by fear. Isaiah 61:1 says:

> The Spirit of the Lord GOD is upon me; because the LORD hath anointed me to preach good tidings unto the meek; he hath sent me to bind up the brokenhearted, to proclaim liberty to the captives, and the opening of the prison to them that are bound;

The people of Ethiopia need Jesus Christ, the Savior of the world. Through Him, their sins can be forgiven, and they can be set free from the bondage of sin and Satan—free in Jesus!

CHAPTER TWELVE

I Didn't Pray, I Begged

Our family went to the United States on furlough in the fall of 1976. The political situation in Ethiopia was deteriorating, and the missionaries were talking about the issues they were facing with the growth of communism. No missionary wanted to leave, and our family was planning to return. Ministries at each mission station were growing. It started to get difficult for the believers as far as religious persecution, and things were getting bad for the missionaries.

Missionaries were busy doing their work, but those living and working in Addis saw more troubling changes happening as communism began to grow and spread. Leaders began to smuggle in a red book by Chairman Mao called *Quotations by Mao Tse-tung*. They were secretly distributing it to the university students. Some went into the forests to study the book together. Haile Selassie opposed sending students abroad to study because they would come back and want to change things in Ethiopia that could not be afforded. The country was still far behind in its infrastructure and education. Many went to Eastern Europe to study, and this is where they learned the communist ideology. The "little red book" was a main factor in spreading communism. As the emperor was getting old, some in the military joined in the efforts to take over the government. They began to work in the various tribal areas to teach communism. They mobilized to teach the university students. There were several small factions fighting each other, but when the army, led by Mengistu Haile Mariam, joined in, things began to move faster. Soon they arrested Haile Selassie and his family.

Sometimes, the university students were sent out to the countryside to teach the communist way. The idea was to take from the rich and give to the poor and make everyone equal. They taught about equal amounts of land and farms, and all this sounded good to some. However, most in the countryside resisted this at first.

Each missionary had their experiences and stories of what they went through. There were curfews at the missionary schools to keep families from being out in the dark. Some who lived off campus would see jeeps with machine guns and were occasionally followed with the intention of intimidating the foreigner. One time, Michael Sidebottom was followed by some military personnel when he drove home on his motorcycle after school. They blocked the road and tried to get him off his motorcycle. They turned it off and basically tried to scare him. They finally let him go, and as he looked back while driving away, they all had their guns aimed at him, but they did not shoot.

The revolution started in the early '70s, and I remember seeing the riots in the city when my parents came to visit us at school. There were protests, and it was a pretty scary thing to see, hear, and experience. I saw signs that said "We hate Americans" and heard the people shout all kinds of things against America, like "Yankees go home!" You couldn't go out as much around Addis as feelings toward Americans started to change. For safety, we had to close the steel gates on the main doors in the front of the student center where some missionaries lived. Protestors threw rocks at the building, and fire trucks came to spray the people to get them under control and away from the building. Sometimes the crowds were big, and on occasion, I could hear gun shots.

Up country was not quite as bad. However, over a couple of years, we went from being loved to being mistrusted. It was just after things were getting bad that we went on furlough.

In April of 1976, the communist government leaders took over the first level of the student center. They put seals on the doors to keep people from entering. They did allow those living there to go in and out. One Sunday morning near the end of May, the government went to the houses behind the student center and told the people to go to an area outside our building for a rally. It became an anti-American and anti-BBFI rally. The mob soon started to move toward the building with the intent to catch anyone they found. They went through the building, but all the missionaries were out at churches, and the few believers who were in the building hid under desks in the offices. One day, there was even a tank that drove down and faced its gun turret at the building to intimidate and cause fear.

Because the situation was getting more dangerous, the missionaries started to sell and give away their personal belongings in the building. The doors were sealed again. The rebels did let them go in to get their things. A few missionaries only got out with a few suitcases and briefcases. They just grabbed the few valuables that they could. The US Embassy obtained permission for the Stampers to get back into the building to get their passports and some clothes. Betty Stamper was pregnant and her doctor and US Embassy officials told them they should leave while the airlines were still providing flights. When they left the building, the crowd that gathered threatened to beat them. They were terrified.

Some missionaries left within five days, and others soon thereafter. It was hard on everyone—even for the kids. Leaving and seeing their parents' hearts broken as they left the people and land they loved was very hard on everyone.

Things were getting tense and extremely dangerous for the believers. Some were shot and many were tortured. The time had come to have the churches meet secretly. Through the Bible institute, the Sidebottoms started to prepare pastors and students for underground or secret services as they saw things getting much worse. They shared and taught the book *Come Wind Come Weather* about the underground church in China. They made copies of the book and gave it to the leaders and students to know how to plan and implement these measures.

Churches began to meet secretly, and as they had their services, the people came one-by-one hours before the service and then afterward would leave one by one or two by two. People were getting saved during those difficult times, and they would perform the baptisms in bathtubs of the houses where they met.

While all this was going on in the city of Addis, the missionaries were trying to figure out what to do with the mission stations. Denton Collins and Jerry Piercey went up to Robi and then Jaraniro and got as much as they could and took it all to Kombolcha to be stored. The Yarnells, who lived in Jaraniro, had gone on furlough in 1975 with hopes of returning. Mo Garner had given money for a bigger generator to run their mission station. It was a diesel generator and could run the entire station, plus the deep freeze and power tools. When Piercey and Collins started to load up the generator to take it to Kombolcha, the people stopped them and said it belonged to them now since communism had come. They talked to them for a while, and the people finally let the missionaries take it.

Groups of young men called the Kebele (Keh-beh-lay) were formed, who went in to teach the people communism and to arrest those who resisted the teaching. They acted as neighborhood administrators and controllers in urban parts of Ethiopia. It wasn't long before they began to speak negatively about the foreigners and missionaries. They also began to threaten them. Even the Italians who had lived there for years and married to Ethiopians were targets of their threats.

When things seemed to be getting worse and even severe, Negatu went to Dad's printing press to get rid of things in case there was anything that could possibly be used against them. We had a building that housed the printing press and offices used by Gordon Wright. Gordon would send correspondence courses around Ethiopia and into Eritrea. Many people took those courses, and quite a few students were then serving in the Ethiopian army.

There was a picture of Haile Selassie in the building, and Negatu got rid of it. Then he came across some stationery that belonged to Duane Baker, a BBFI missionary who had left Ethiopia several years previously. He left his stationery to be used as scratch paper for writing up lessons and for test printing. On one side of the letterhead was a picture of their family, and on other side a picture or old map of Ethiopia. The map was so old that Eritrea was not shown on the map, since it had belonged to the Italians years before. At that time, however, Eritrea was trying to become its own country and break away from being a province of Ethiopia, which it eventually succeeded in doing. If the authorities found this stationery with the old map on it, they could have accused Dad and the other missionaries of being anti-Ethiopia and pro-Eritrea.

Negatu decided to give this stationery to some of the older school students for them to tear off the top of the letterhead. They were to burn the top part with the map and keep the rest for scratch paper. Two of them were boys I grew up with and knew well. In the process, several of the papers with the letterhead blew away. Another friend of mine, Iyalio, found it and turned it in to the authorities not knowing where it had come from and therefore not knowing who would get into trouble. Turning it in to the authorities led to the officials going to the mission station in a truck, and they arrested all the workers, teachers, and Negatu. They were accused of being conspirators with the "foreigner," and therefore of treason, and incarcerated in an old Italian stone prison.

The Lackeys, fairly new BBFI missionaries, lived on the Kombolcha mission station at that time and knew they would have to leave soon. Things had become very tense, and authorities demanded to go through everything. The Lackeys eventually left after they endured some threatening times of mental abuse and fear of arrest. All of this took place while we were on furlough.

After storing many things at the Kombolcha mission station from the other stations, Denton Collins called my dad who was in America and said that most of the others were leaving, and he wanted to know what to do with our things. Dad said he was planning to return, which he did soon thereafter. Dad obtained his reentry permit in record time—three days. When he got back to Addis, Denton drove Dad twelve hours north in Jerry Piercey's black Suburban SUV to check out the situation in Kombolcha. Communism had taken over Haik, and they disbanded everything associated with the mission station there. The Morrows were living and ministering in Haik, but they had already left the country.

When Denton and Dad arrived in Kombolcha, they realized things were not good, and there was no way we could return there as a family to live and continue ministry. It was upon their arrival that they found out that Negatu, the teachers, and workers had been arrested, so they decided to sell all our belongings. There was very little left in the house where the other missionaries had lived. The local town and village people were told that everything we had was going to be sold.

The rebel youth came to church in town one day and enthusiastically told Dad all the good things about communism. Dad asked them to give an example of where this idea had worked for the good in the world. They responded Tanzania. In those days, Tanzania was socialist, but it was not working. The people did not have much to eat and had very little work. The Tanzanians would go to Kenya to get supplies. Then they said Russia. They were very brainwashed and really did not know what they were talking about.

For the next three days, people came to buy things. People came from all over to buy our belongings. Dad was trying to sell everything in order to give a severance pay to the workers. At times, the people became somewhat hostile, and they started to take things and run off. One day, Asefa said to Dad, "This is too much of a strain on you. I will sell things for you while you go to Boromeda for some rest." So Dad and Denton left for a few hours. When they returned, Asefa was frustrated and uneasy and said, "I can't do this anymore. These people are like wild people." They tore off the screen door and tried to push their way into the house. There were two men among the crowd who stirred the people up. Everyone dispersed, and the people went away. After a little while, the people came back to apologize and said, "We don't know why we have acted this way. You are our friend, and you have done so much for us." A few hours later, the local people turned into mad people again. This went on for three days.

At the end of those three days, a pickup truck showed up with a load of young men and an army officer. They said, "We have come to arrest you because we believe you are here as an enemy of the country." They went into the house and rifled through things in each room. When they were done in each room, they placed a piece of paper with glue over the door as a seal for the government and said, "You cannot go in there."

Dad received a notification to report to a certain office in town because he was accused by one of the men who worked for Gordon Wright. This man oversaw the night schools and took care of the mules. He accused Dad of trying to leave the country and neglecting to care for the animals. Dad had to figure out how to get to town because the officials had said that his car could not be used—neither the Land Rover nor the SUV. He finally found a ride, and when he got there, the accusation was read aloud before the head official who was over these types of matters. When it was done being read, the officer in charge got upset with the Ethiopian worker and said, "We don't care about these animals. We aren't interested in them. Let the hyenas eat them." So Dad was released and got a ride back to the station. Upon arrival, he noticed some of the furniture was gone. Somebody had stolen it. It was a crazy time and mentally taxing working through all these situations. Eventually, Dad sold most of our belongings, and the rest was stolen.

For eleven days, Dad and Denton were under this pressure of false accusations and house arrest. The people did not understand all that was going on because of all the false propaganda against the foreigners and the missionaries. During those days of house arrest in Kombolcha, there was no communication with Mom. She did not know what was happening.

Some of our close Ethiopian friends who appreciated my parents and all they did for the community brought food daily for Dad and Denton to eat. When the local Kebele (youth neighborhood administrators) heard about this, they told the people to stop feeding them. Then the village farmers who had guns were designated as the guards over the missionaries, day and night. The prisoners could not go anywhere, and no one could bring them food. Eventually, the Italian family who had a gas station and restaurant was granted permission to bring them one meal a day. That family was also preparing to leave. They were accused of being against the government. They had lived there most of their lives.

In the beginning, Dad and Denton had liberty to move around if they stayed inside the station. The first pioneer unit we lived in had become the storage place, and it had a lot of the Yarnells's things that had been transported for safekeeping. Dad also had barrels under our house that belonged to the Wrights. He didn't know what was in them. He and Denton were afraid of what could be found in the other missionaries' stored boxes and barrels.

Eventually, Dad and Denton were restricted to the house, and they slept on the floor. They were told, "Don't leave the house. We know a helicopter will come from over the mountain and pick you up and take you away to America." They had seen some helicopters in years past with the Mapping Mission, mapping out the roads of Ethiopia, so they thought it was possible. Once, while eating, Dad got a little sick and had to go to the restroom. We only had the outhouse. It was raining, and the guards were relaxing. Dad ran outside to the outhouse in the rain. The guards saw him running down the path, so they rushed into the house to Denton and said, "Where did he go?" pointing their guns at him. He said, "To the bathroom." They said, "No he didn't. He ran to the field because a helicopter is coming from America to get him." Just then, Dad returned to the house, and the guards were very upset. The local people who were now guards didn't understand things but were just doing what they were told to do.

Dad began thinking about how Lyle always hunted and thought, "Oh my, those guns are down there in his things in storage." The people were going through the buildings looking for things to use to accuse the men of working for the CIA. Dad surely did not want them to find those guns, which would cause a huge problem. The men found some of Lyle Yarnell's things that had gun shell loaders and ammunition. They devised a plan to get rid of those things.

Denton planned to sneak the gun powder out and spread it in the yard by acting as though he was going for a walk and praying. He shook his pant legs from time to time, dropping the gun powder on the grass and walked back over it to push it down. While Denton walked around the yard with the gun powder, Dad walked in another area of the yard closer to the fence. Every time they went to the outhouse, they put shells in their pockets and threw them down the hole. They were so fearful of what these guys might do, so they did this very carefully. If they were caught, they would have been taken to prison. Dad really wanted to take the loader down to the river and throw it in, but he never got the chance. Instead, he walked near the fence along a ditch and threw it in there, praying no one would find it until after they were released and gone. During this house arrest, missionary John Flynn occasionally got the mail and took it to Dad.

When they went through the Wright's things, they found barrels filled with old Baptist Bible Tribunes, papers, and books, but nothing that would cause a problem. They went to the pioneer unit and didn't find much except another rifle. They tried to think of a plan to deal with that. Dad couldn't tell the guards about it because they would accuse him of hiding it and not turning it in at the beginning. So he took the rifle apart and tried to figure out how to dispose of it. Dad looked around and found a toy saw that he thought might be useful. He built a fire in the fireplace, then he cut the rifle stock up into squares with the toy plastic saw. Imagine the difficulty of cutting that hardwood with a toy saw, plus the fear of guards finding him on that task. He took the wood pieces and burned them in the fireplace.

Then one night, he took apart the barrel of the gun and the scope. He sneaked out through the fence and threw the scope out into the field. On the school ground, we had an outhouse with a deep hole. Later that night, Dad crept out and hid from the guards, running behind bushes and buildings with the gun barrel down his pant leg. It was hard to run with it while he held the barrel with his hand in his pocket. He made it up to that outhouse and threw the barrel down the hole. What a relief it was to get rid of that without getting caught.

Denton had an employee in Addis named Joseph. The man had not heard from Denton while he was in Kombolcha. This concerned Joseph, so he got on a bus to Kombolcha to find out what had happened. When he arrived at the mission station, he was arrested also and held for several days. Joseph was finally released, and he returned to Addis on the bus.

Dad was allowed once to visit the workers in prison. The only food they were given was food that family members brought to them. The workers were not allowed to wear shoes, making it harder for them to run away. If they tried to escape, the guards would use sticks to beat the bottoms of their feet until they were so swollen they couldn't walk. Most of them behaved and were not mistreated as badly. Some families brought food with tracts hidden inside. The tracts were distributed to other prisoners. When the guards found out, they started to put their hands in the food to find those tracts. The tracts stopped coming, but the ones that initially made it through were used to lead other prisoners to Christ.

The local leaders decided Denton and Dad would have to go to the capital city because the Ministry of Security was looking at them as spies. Dad packed three barrels of stuff he wanted to ship back to the United States. He put them inside the back of Jerry Piercey's SUV. They traveled with two armed guards. One guard sat with his rifle next to Denton in the front as Denton drove. Dad was in the back next to another guard with a rifle. There were a lot of roadblocks, with guards pretty much at every town. This was because there was a lot going on against the government. So at these roadblocks, the police would normally go through everything in each vehicle. In a way, it was a blessing to have the two guards with them because when the police saw these guards and heard the foreign prisoners were wanted by the Ministry of Security, they got to go through all the roadblocks without having each item searched. They only had personal things in them, but you never knew how officials would try to twist even innocent items and accuse you of something else.

While Dad and Denton were under city arrest in Addis, awaiting a verdict from the highest court concerning their accusation of being spies, Negatu and the teachers back in Kombolcha were taken into the center of town and accused of working with the enemy. They were placed before a mob of one hundred people who were shouting, "Hang them! Hang them!" It was getting very tense, and the crowd was getting closer around them ready to do it. The authorities just stood by and watched. But a man spoke up and said, "Let's wait before hanging them. Let's put them back in prison and see what the authorities in Addis do with those foreigners. If they do something to those foreigners, then we will hang them." The mob backed off and followed this person's advice and dispersed.

For a few months in Addis, Dad dealt with the false accusation pretty much every day. He stayed in Denton's house because the student center was now closed. He slept on the floor since the Collins family had already gotten rid of most of their things preparing to leave. Dad had already purchased his return plane tickets. However, officials had confiscated his passport. Every day Dad walked to the Ministry of Security and asked them what the judgment of the ruling military committee was concerning them. They always responded by saying, "The committee is very busy." Outside of the Ministry of Security, there was a huge granite rock that was seven feet in diameter. Every day, Dad would leave the building, drape himself over that rock, and pray and weep.

People today often ask Dad if he prayed a lot during those times. He says, "No, I begged and wept, pleading for God to intervene." Sure, he prayed, but it was more than a casual prayer. Some foreigners had been arrested, and some died before being released. Many Ethiopians died even though falsely accused. Officials would just shoot them and let the hyenas eat them. As he walked to the government office and back to Denton's house, Dad saw dead people's bodies stacked up like firewood on the side of the street. They could not be buried until the family had paid the government a fee for the bullet used to kill them. These were serious and dangerous times.

There was no communication with Mom during those three months. Dad heard the US State Department was interested in them, but they really did nothing to help their serious situation. The US Embassy was on low staff, and the ambassador was gone. When Dad got to see the embassy officials, he told them what he had gone through with the Ministry of Security. They threw up hands and said, "Don't cause any problems. We can't help you." However, they did eventually notify the State Department in Washington, DC, about Dad's accusation and pending court ruling. That is when the State Department did locate and communicate with Mom in Denver.

I remember her receiving the call when they notified her that Dad had been arrested and accused of being with the CIA. They mentioned he was now in Addis waiting for the final ruling on his case. Mom gathered us around and informed us of the call. She didn't cry at that moment, but later I heard her inside her bedroom crying and praying. This was the first she knew about what was going on, and it was not good news. How would the ruling committee rule on his case? Would he make it out alive? Would we ever see him again? We all felt helpless, but we prayed!

The government began to persecute the believers and church leaders. In other parts of the country, some terrible things were happening to Christians because of their faith. Government officials put nails through boards and beat their backs, tearing the flesh if they did not deny Jesus. Ladies had their babies taken away from them, sometimes for months, if they did not deny Christ. They would respond, "I love my child, but I cannot deny Jesus my Savior." Eventually, their children would be brought back to them. Pastors were buried alive in fields with their heads out of the ground. Horses were then ridden through the fields, mutilating the heads of those pastors with the horses' hoofs. It was a horrific and terrifying time for believers.

The highest military court finally ruled insufficient evidence and absolved Dad and Denton from having done anything wrong. Dad's passport was returned to him. Against the wishes of Denton, Dad got on a bus and went back to Kombolcha to see the leaders released and to finish selling things, especially the Land Rover. Dad wanted to pay those left behind what he could and what they deserved. All the teachers and workers were released because Dad was released. However, the government informed Negatu that he had to leave Kombolcha since he was the pastor. He moved to Addis. His family was to remain in Kombolcha. He did not see them for four years while he was gone. Negatu began to work as an evangelist secretly with the church cell groups in the capital city.

The churches in Addis began meeting secretly in homes, and Negatu would go to those places to teach and encourage the church members. The church leaders were thankful for his help and wisdom during these very difficult times. People would go into homes at night two or three at a time. Their children would stay outside in the yard to play. There was no singing but only teaching. After the teaching was done, they would leave a few people at a time. A few more would then arrive. They did this every night. The neighbors would turn them in if they found out what was going on.

Upon hearing of Dad's return to Kombolcha, the Kebele youth went to ask what he was doing back there. Dad told them he had been released and the accusations absolved. They were angry and said, "We will see about that." Well, they found out it was true. They had such vengeance and hatred which made the days there very intense.

The time came to sell the Land Rover. The village people said Dad couldn't sell it. They said it belonged to them now because their local leaders told them that anything that belonged to the foreigner was now theirs. They said, "The Land Rover is now ours, and we need it to take people to and from the hospital in the next town." Dad said, "None of you know how to drive it, and I need to sell it to pay the workers their severance pay." They said, "No you can't sell it. We will find someone to drive it, or we will teach someone to drive it." This became a big issue for several days. Some people from Boromeda came because they heard about the sale of the car. Among them was an Ethiopian nurse who said he would like to buy it. Dad said, "They won't let me sell it to you or to anyone." The nurse spent all afternoon speaking with the people, and finally they agreed it could be sold to him. He made it into a bus to transport people to other towns. There was a lot of tension through all of this.

Finally, the car was sold, and all the workers and teachers were paid their severance. Dad felt good about that. However, now he had to find a way back to Addis. He needed to get back to catch his flight out before Denton left the country.

Dad went into town the day his Land Rover was sold, looking for transportation back to Addis. He thought of the Italian, Senior Rosmo. He did not speak much English. However, he understood the situation and knew how bad things were getting, so he offered to take Dad back to Addis when ready. The only thing was that Dad needed to supply the gas for the twelve-hour drive. Gas was being rationed at that time, so it was hard to get enough to make a trip like that. Dad said he did not think he had enough, but he would check. He went back to the mission station. Next to the toolshed were three fifty-five-gallon barrels. They kept one with kerosene for lanterns and the refrigerator, one with diesel for the generator, and one with gas for the vehicles and such.

Dad had already checked them when he first returned. He remembered there was no diesel, a little kerosene, and no gas. He was very discouraged and didn't know what to do. He prayed and asked God to somehow intervene and provide the way. About fifteen minutes later, he was talking with Ababa. Ababa sensed Dad's discouragement and asked if he could help. Dad explained the situation with needing to get to Addis and needing to supply the fuel, but that there was none in the barrels. Ababa told him there was gas in one barrel. Dad said, "No, I already checked it before." Ababa was adamant that there was some. Dad told him he already checked. Ababa was persistent about it, so they went to the barrels and looked. When they opened the gas barrel, it was three-quarters full—just the right amount needed for the trip. God had answered Dad's prayer and miraculously provided the fuel needed to make it to Addis.

When Dad was leaving Kombolcha for the last time, he was very depressed and felt like their time had been wasted. Asefa said to him, "We don't want you to go, but we know you have to go. I want you to know that your time in Ethiopia has not been a waste. If you had not come, I would not have heard of Jesus and trusted Him as my Savior."

Teferra was the tailor in Jaraniro that Lyle Yarnell had led to the Lord and trained. He loved the Lord and wanted to see the work continue even after the missionaries left. With Negatu being ordered to move to Addis, the church needed a leader to help them through the next years. Teferra went to Kombolcha and helped that church survive through the revolution and communism. He is still there as a leader in the church.

Dad was in Addis for a few days before he left. He had a plane ticket to leave on a Saturday. An Egyptian family, the Khalils, let him stay with them on Friday night. The reason Denton didn't want Dad to go back to Kombolcha was because he had plans to secretly evacuate the emperor's grandkids. Denton had been miraculously given custody of those grandkids. He wanted Dad to be out of Ethiopia for his safety. Denton said, "Richard, I can't tell you everything, but when it comes time to leave, I am leaving. We have two planes coming to Lake Langano, and they will be taking the grandchildren to Kenya. Sorry, but there is no room for you. You must get out of the country before this happens."

Dad left on that Saturday as planned. The next day on Sunday morning, Denton took Jerry's truck down to the lakeside with the grandchildren. That afternoon, two planes arrived on the shoreline of the lake and carried them away to safety in Kenya. Joseph, who went up to check on them in Kombolcha, also left for southern Ethiopia out of fear for his own life. He knew of this plan, and that was dangerous for him.

Dad took on the plane two suitcases that contained personal pictures and a few clothes. He also carried a little bookshelf that held cookbooks I had made in boarding school. When Dad left on the plane, he said he didn't cry any tears, but he just stared silently out the window at the land below as they took off. It was as if there were no more tears to cry. He knew God had called them there. In fact, Mom and Dad had picked out a place under a big tree on the church grounds in Kombolcha, where they planned to be buried. It was hard for them to leave their home, and it broke their hearts wondering why this had happened. Their church had really grown before all this took place. There was sadness for the believers, and Dad hated to leave them behind. He understood, though, that it was best for their safety. The believers in Kombolcha had reluctantly told him he needed to leave.

The plane he left on flew to Kenya. Some of the missionaries had gone to live in Kenya, including the Herrings and Hokansons. The Hokansons took care of Dad for a few days before he flew to the United States. It was in Kenya that Dad first communicated with Mom after more than three months. While in Kenya, Dad met with Denton at a hotel. He never saw the emperor's grandchildren, and Denton did not speak about them. He and Jodi Collins had set up this plan for their escape with few people knowing about it.

While we were on furlough, all together again, Dad began to work on his master's degree from Azusa Pacific College in California. While there, we took a trip to San Francisco. One of the main reasons was to take a tour of Alcatraz. While on the tour, Mom looked all around and pointed things out to us. When we got to the housing area for the guards, the tour guide asked if anyone had been to Alcatraz before.

Mom raised her hand. He said, "Oh, I am sure you were here on a tour before?" She said, "No, I used to live here." You can imagine the amazed response from the entire group after that.

This may be the end of this story, but it is not the end of the story of the Konnerup family in Africa. Stay tuned for the next installment to see where God leads them and continues to use them.

About the Author

Jonathan Konnerup was born in Addis Ababa, Ethiopia. His parents, Richard and Jeannine Konnerup, were pioneer missionaries in Ethiopia from 1960 until communism took control of the country in the mid-1970s. Then they moved to Kenya, East Africa, when Jonathan was in high school, where he attended the Rift Valley Academy. He attended Liberty University where he met his wife, Pam, where both were studying to be missionaries. They were approved as Baptist Bible Fellowship International missionaries to Kenya in May of 1987 and arrived in September of 1988. Several churches and a Bible college were started under their ministry. Their daughter, Bethany, was born in 1993 in Nairobi, Kenya, and today works as a registered nurse. The Konnerups served in Kenya until Jonathan became an associate mission director for the BBFI in July of 1998. Since May of 2005, Jonathan Konnerup has served as Mission Director of the BBFI.